LLOYD WRIGHT

THE ARCHITECTURE OF FRANK LLOYD WRIGHT JR.

LLOYD WRIGHT
THE ARCHITECTURE OF FRANK LLOYD WRIGHT JR.

PRODUCED AND PHOTOGRAPHED BY
ALAN WEINTRAUB

ESSAY BY THOMAS S. HINES

REMEMBRANCE BY ERIC LLOYD WRIGHT

TEXTS BY DANA HUTT

HARRY N. ABRAMS, INC., PUBLISHERS

ENDPAPERS Pine-tree concrete-block motif, Johnson House, Los Angeles, 1963
TITLE PAGE Wayfarer's Chapel, Palos Verdes, 1946–51
CONTENTS PAGE Lloyd Wright, 1962
PAGE 276 Lloyd Wright, 1975

Designed by Zand Gee
Edited by Cathryn Drake

Library of Congress Cataloging-in-Publication Data

Wright, Lloyd, 1890–1978.
    Lloyd Wright : the architecture of Frank Lloyd Wright Jr. /
produced and photographed by Alan Weintraub; essays by Thomas S.
Hines, Eric Lloyd Wright; house texts by Dana Hutt.
        p.   cm.
    Includes bibliographical references.
    ISBN 0-8109-3996-7 (hardcover)
    1. Wright, Lloyd, 1890–1978—Themes, motives. 2. Architecture,
Domestic—California, Southern. I. Weintraub, Alan. II. Hines,
Thomas S. III. Wright, Eric Lloyd. IV. Title.
    NA737.W72A4   1998a
    720'.92—dc21   98-25052

Copyright © 1998 Alan Weintraub

First published in Great Britain in 1998 by Thames and Hudson Ltd, London

Published in 1998 by Harry N. Abrams, Incorporated, New York.

Printed and bound in Singapore

Harry N. Abrams, Inc.
100 Fifth Avenue
New York, N.Y. 10011
www.abramsbooks.com

To my father, Semon Weintraub

CONTENTS

FOREWORD

My fascination with modern residential architecture first revealed itself when I was a small child and my art teacher asked me to draw a picture of my own house. The result looked more like a futuristic series of floating horizontal boxes than it did my New England Colonial three-bedroom home. Perhaps as a result of this early effort and the endless

Frank Lloyd Wright. Perspective drawing, Millard House, Pasadena, California, 1923

series of odd house drawings that followed, my father returned home one evening with four books, one of which was *The Architecture of Frank Lloyd Wright*, by Vincent Scully. Flipping through the pages, I came upon a rendering of the Millard house in Pasadena, California. At that moment my life took a major turn as I realized that a house didn't have to look like a "house." Some decades and thousands of drawings later—after extensive architectural studies—I opted for a career in residential architectural photography. I soon began compiling an archive of unusual houses, focusing on works by architects who had been overlooked, ignored, or forgotten despite or because of their unorthodox designs.

In the late 1980s my friend and client Steve Badanes of Jersey Devil Architects/Builders invited me to visit the Malibu ranch of Eric Lloyd Wright, grandson of Frank Lloyd Wright. Steve was assisting with the concrete work required for the construction of an astounding cliff-top house on the property. During this visit I told Eric how much I admired a house in Hollywood that I had assumed was designed by his grandfather. He replied that the Sowden house was in fact designed by his father, Lloyd Wright, an architect whose work had been underappreciated. I was surprised that the son of such a renowned architect had gained so little recognition, but was delighted to learn that there was an archive of his designs for residential, landscape, and civic architecture.

Armed with the limited literature on Lloyd Wright consisting of a small monograph by David Gebhard and Harriette Von Breton and an article in the Japanese magazine *Space Design,* along with Eric's own

photographs and the Lloyd Wright archives at the UCLA research library, I began taking Polaroid photos of each house, noting the addresses and original owners in my new red notebook. This was the beginning of ten years of research on and photography of every extant Lloyd Wright building—and the conception of this book.

Soon after the project began to develop, I was photographing an article for *Architectural Digest* in Los Angeles. I mentioned the book to the associate editor of architecture, Lucas Dietrich, who recognized the importance of my research. Thus began his intense involvement with the work presented in this book. Lucas asked Professor Thomas Hines of the UCLA Architecture Department to write an article on Lloyd Wright for the magazine, which would be accompanied by my photographs.

Later Lucas and I visited the Department of Special Collections at the UCLA research library, where we noticed a young woman in the reading room who was researching the work of Lloyd Wright. But it was not until several years later at a symposium on Lloyd Wright at Eric Wright's ranch that I met Dana Hutt, who as a graduate student had been writing her thesis on Wright when I had observed her in the library. Both Dana and I were on the symposium panel, and I was so impressed by her knowledge of Wright that I asked her right then if she would write the house texts for the book. Dana had been busy researching two major architecture exhibitions for The Museum of Contemporary Art, Los Angeles, but was eager to be involved in the project. And I knew of no one else who had a better command of the material.

I had already asked Professor Hines to expand his article on Lloyd Wright to a biographical essay for the book. Eric agreed to write a personal essay about his father; and my longtime friend, fellow photographer, and graphic designer Zand Gee agreed to design the book. The team was assembled: each an expert in their respective fields about to embark on a journey in which we would all learn more than perhaps anyone in the world about the long-neglected architect.

Meanwhile Lucas had left *Architectural Digest* and moved to London to become the architecture editor at the publisher Thames and Hudson. After several years, more than 4,000 photographs, and a preliminary design layout, I proposed the book to publishers in four countries, which began a series of highs and lows regarding the extent of control and completeness with which I would be allowed to present the work. Lucas fought hard, and in the end it was Thames and Hudson who agreed to publish the complete work of Lloyd Wright.

Sitting here in a Paris café, I feel that I have just signed an agreement with the most appropriate publisher for the work, bringing to full circle a project that has taken ten years to complete. More than anyone, I thank Eric Lloyd Wright, without whose interest, enthusiasm, time, and invaluable assistance this book would not have been possible. I also thank Eric's wife, Mary, and sons, Devon and Cory, an incredibly warm and wonderful family whose love and devotion to one another and their extended family have helped to make this book a real tribute to Lloyd Wright. Thanks to the associates at the studio of Eric Lloyd Wright— Karen, Ralph, Francis, and John—for their assistance throughout the endless phone calls and requests for materials and information. My appreciation extends to Lloyd Wright's stepson, Rupert Pole, who contributed valuable information and was a pleasure to get to know during the course of my research.

I would like to extend my deepest thanks to Steve Badanes, who lit the initial fire that culminated with this book, and especially to Zand Gee, who has worked closely with me for the past three years organizing the material for this project. Many thanks to Thomas Hines, Dana Hutt, and my project editor, Cathryn Drake, all of whom have probably spent more time and energy than they ever expected on this book.

I am grateful for the longtime support of David Weingarten, architect-critic Alan Hess, and author Diane Dorrans Saeks, who have stood by me throughout the years of ups and downs surrounding this project.

A very special thank-you to my friend and editor Lucas Dietrich, David Morton, photographers Julius Shulman and Steven Brooke, Abrams publishers in New York, and the Graham Foundation in Chicago. And of course nothing would have been possible without the cooperation and involvement of the Lloyd Wright building owners—I thank them all for their enthusiastic encouragement and support in letting me return to photograph their homes over and over throughout the years. I would like to note that the houses were photographed "as is" from 1988 to 1998, including any renovations, additions, and changes in decor not only from the original plans but also between visits as some houses changed ownership. I have tried to include as many archival photographs as possible to show the buildings as they were originally intended.

I owe a special acknowledgment to the Los Angeles boxing promoter whose name I don't know and whose wife returned my red notebook after it fell off the top of my car in front of the Mace house. I thank my mother and late father, Bertha and Semon Weintraub, whose support over the years has enabled me to establish the career leading to this book.

This book is for all of you and my friends with whom I have shared my stories and experiences during the past ten years.

Alan Weintraub
January 13, 1998
Paris

THE BLESSING AND THE CURSE

The Achievement of Lloyd Wright by Thomas S. Hines

Lloyd Wright at Wayfarer's Chapel, 1976

ABOVE: Lloyd Wright at Wayfarer's Chapel, 1976 LEFT: Flora Tobin (LW's maternal grandmother), Rosamund Parrish (LW's maternal great-grandmother), Lloyd at age 2, Catherine Tobin Wright (LW's mother), c.1892

In 1978, at Lloyd Wright's funeral in his own Wayfarer's Chapel in Palos Verdes, his niece, the actress Anne Baxter, read Dylan Thomas's poem "Do Not Go Gentle Into That Good Night." It spoke to the central factor in Lloyd's long and significant life: his relationship with his famous father, Frank Lloyd Wright, in whose shadow he had always stood, but from whom he had also gotten his essential education: "And you my father, there on the sad height," it concluded, "curse, bless me now with your fierce tears I pray." Cursed and blessed by that filial–paternal relationship, despite and because of that hovering presence, Lloyd produced great architecture and made important contributions to the physical and cultural landscape, particularly that of southern California, where he lived the greatest part of his life. There, throughout the twentieth century, he and other avant-garde architects courageously explored the fertile intersection of modernism and regionalism.[1]

Lloyd (LW) never doubted that his superhuman father was a greater presence than he was, not only in the field of architecture but in the realms of ideas and communications. He acknowledged that Frank Lloyd Wright (FLW) was a greater designer, thinker, speaker, and writer than he was. And he knew that FLW surpassed him in messianic zeal, the realm that Lloyd referred to as "preaching": "One of the most remarkable things about my father," he once told an interviewer, "was that he was not only a damn good architect and visualizer . . . but he was a good preacher. . . . He both preached and did. And he built and preached. He built what he preached."[2]

Aside from the reflected glory of being the son of Frank Lloyd Wright, Lloyd stood on his own as an impressive architect and human being. No one caught this better than the writer Anaïs Nin, the longtime companion of Lloyd's stepson, Rupert Pole. In her famous and controversial diaries, Nin recorded the impressions of her first visit to the architect's home: "I saw first of all a high wall, like the wall of a medieval castle," she wrote. "And a giant tree, which seemed to extend its ancient branches to keep the house from prying eyes. . . . For the first time in many years in America, I entered a home where beauty reigned, in a world created entirely by an artist." She followed this reverie with an evocation of the man himself and of his wife Helen. "Over six feet tall, gray hair, a full round head with a very high forehead, laughing eyes, and an emotional mouth," she said of Lloyd. "He has a powerful voice, gracious manners, a hearty laugh. Next to him a tiny woman with a very sweet voice, sea-blue eyes, large and melting with softness . . . who was an actress and now gives dramatic readings of plays."[3]

For Nin, "Lloyd's presence gave a feeling of power. The sensitivity I saw later, when he took me to his office and showed me his drawings and projects, and models for future buildings. His drawings were very beautiful in themselves, the concepts absolutely original and poetic. That was the first word which came to my mind. . . . He is the poet of architecture. For him a building, a home, a stone, a roof, every inch of architecture has meaning . . . a triumph over the monotony and homeliness which I had seen from New York throughout the Middle West, in every city."[4]

Though always known as Lloyd to distinguish him from his father, Frank Lloyd Wright Jr. was born March 31, 1890, in Oak Park, Illinois. Based upon interviews with the architect, historians David Gebhard and Harriette Von Breton evoked the impact of Lloyd's childhood environment in their pathbreaking 1971 exhibition and catalogue at the University of California, Santa Barbara. "Lloyd was not in rebellion against his father's radical directions nor his integrity of spirit and purpose," Von Breton observed. "He was nurtured in an environment designed by his father . . . with a full accompaniment of vocal, audio, and visual enrichment that was part of his father's credo."[5]

Lloyd's mother, Catherine, ran a kindergarten at home for her children and for those of neighbors and friends. There Lloyd was introduced to the world of Friedrich Froebel, whose chunky building blocks and colorful geometric paper patterns influenced his spatial imagination, as they had the senior Wright a generation earlier. Later, like his father, he studied with his great aunts, Jane and Nell Lloyd-Jones, at their Hillside Home School in Spring Green, Wisconsin, where he imbibed the rural beauty of his family's ancestral landscape. He recorded his appreciation of its natural wonders in a short poem written at Hillside when he was about ten, which demonstrated at this early age his concern for the problem of the good and beautiful surviving and triumphing over the violent and hostile:

I walked upon the hill one day
To rocky ledges far away
And there from out the warming ground
A wind-blown fur-cloaked flower found.
Its sturdy stalk upheld a cup
Whose azure-tinted face turned up
Drank in the vigor of the light
And gave it back in beauty bright.

Oh, little flower whose power for good
Has triumphed over wind and flood.
Would that I might have thy power
To triumph over wind and shower.[6]

Along with nature and Froebel's geometric exercises, music was a constant in Lloyd's education, cultivating in him a sensitivity that would prove beneficial to his later designs for the Hollywood Bowl and for such clients as the violinist Jascha Heifetz. He played cello in the family chamber orchestra and was especially touched by his father's impromptu piano recitals: "Father used to play Bach and Beethoven at night," he recounted, "and I can remember listening to the music while I was a small boy night after night in my cot. He used to play it like his heart would break."[7]

This recalled a similar and equally plaintive memory by FLW of his own father, William Wright: "Father sometimes played the piano far into the night, and much of Beethoven and Bach the boy learned by heart as he lay listening. Living seemed a kind of listening to him—then. Sometimes it was as though a door would open and he would get the beautiful meaning clear. Then it would close and the meaning would be dim or far away. But there was always some meaning. Father taught him to see a symphony as an edifice—of sound."[8]

Lloyd also inherited his father's taste for Oriental rugs, Japanese prints, and the furniture and accoutrements of the Arts and Crafts movement, as well as the designs and artifacts of pre-Columbian Mexican and Southwestern American Indian culture. He had grown up among these objects in the Oak Park house. In the late 1930s Lloyd would confirm the importance of these legacies: "Had the Japanese prints out the other evening for a review," he wrote his father. "It was a refreshing experience. I don't know why I haven't done it oftener. Stimulating as a spring shower." In 1948 he acknowledged with delight a gift from his father of "a very fine red Indian bowl. We are enjoying its beautiful contours and good red color."[9]

Throughout his early years Lloyd also absorbed the esprit and intensity of the Oak Park studio, learning by observing not only FLW but such gifted associates as William Drummond and Marion Mahony Griffin. By his midteens he had become an accomplished draftsman. In 1907 Lloyd enrolled at his father's alma mater, the University of Wisconsin, Madison, majoring in engineering and agronomy, playing in chamber music groups, and rowing on the college crew. He

ABOVE: Lloyd Wright rendering of American System-Built House designed by FLW, 1916
LEFT: Lloyd in his 30s, c.1920

remained for only two years, slightly longer than his father did, but garnered knowledge from his double major that would later serve him well in both architecture and landscaping.

In 1909, following Ralph Waldo Emerson's admonition against "conforming to usages that are dead to you," FLW left his wife, family, and architectural practice in Oak Park and eloped to Italy with his lover, a former client, Mamah Borthwick Cheney. Establishing a small studio in Fiesole, Wright, with a small staff that included Lloyd, prepared the elegant drawings of his Prairie School buildings for publication by the German firm Wasmuth. The resulting book and folio would have a large impact on the next generation of European modernists.

Following this arduous but satisfying assignment, Lloyd traveled with Taylor Woolley, a fellow draftsman, around Italy, France, and Germany. Europe opened new vistas to Lloyd in architecture, and particularly in landscape design, and quickened his resolve to pursue those fields on his own. By 1911 neither he nor his father had sufficient funds to allow him to return to college. Instead he moved to Boston, where he worked briefly at the Harvard Herbarium before joining the prestigious landscape firm Olmsted and Olmsted. This position allowed him to transfer in fall 1911 to San Diego, where the Olmsteds had established a nursery to develop plantings for the Pan-Pacific Exposition, scheduled to open in 1915. His brother John, also a budding architect, accompanied him there. California appealed greatly to Lloyd and, except for another brief sojourn to the East Coast, he remained there for the rest of his life. His favorite buildings in San Diego were those by Irving Gill, with whom FLW had been a fellow apprentice, and briefly a supervisor, in Louis Sullivan's Chicago office in the early 1890s.

In 1912, because of a strained relationship with exposition officials over the siting of buildings, the Olmsteds resigned their appointment in Balboa Park. They were also upset with the appointment of Bertram Goodhue as chief designer instead of Gill, who had worked to secure their appointment and who, they had assumed, would design the fair. Lloyd apparently could have remained on the exposition staff, but he elected not to do so.

After staying for a brief time to help with the plantings, he resigned and joined Gill, "a good sound man with ideas and ideals," he wrote FLW. "He is, to say the least, appreciative of your work. . . . To the inspiration he gained at that time, he lays a great deal of his success." Gill had offered Lloyd a job in which he "would turn over all of his clients' landscape work to me, give me a desk in his office, all the materials and aids I needed with free rein to handle the matter as I saw fit. With the proviso . . . that I received my pay when I made the department pay. Don't laugh and say that I was a silly ass for taking it for I am not. I know what lies in this particular job, I know what an opportunity is, and I seized it. I have been in the work head over heels for the last week. I have already had two propositions handed to me to lay out and handle and more in view. . . . I wouldn't let the opportunity slip [by] me without giving it a good six months tryout for anything in the world. It will mean the making of me if I can hang on."[10] Ultimately Lloyd's importance to Gill proved to be not only in his effective landscaping but in the beautiful presentation renderings he did of Gill's buildings.

Lloyd then thanked FLW for his offer to pay for his continued cello lessons but reported that he had found no suitable teacher in San Diego and that he might instead need to call on his father for more basic provisions in the months ahead. He continued his letter by conveying Gill's greetings, despite the latter's fear that FLW would not remember him. Lloyd then quoted Gill's confession that "still you are as vivid a character to him as when he saw you last some twenty years ago. He is so interested that he has asked if you would favor him with one of your photos." This also seemed important to Lloyd as a way of confirming his boss's commitment to keep him. He closed his letter with the jocular plea "Get on the elevator if you will and help shove; we're going up."[11]

In the early part of the century Gill had built several experimental cottages in the Hillcrest district of San Diego, targeted for working-class budgets. The architect had lived in several of the cottages. When Lloyd joined his office, his employer allowed him and his brother John to live for free in one of the houses. "Gill looked after me like a son," Lloyd later recalled.

The largest project in Gill's office in those years was the design, undertaken jointly with the Olmsteds, for the industrial city of Torrance, south of Los Angeles. Lloyd designed and supervised the planting of both the central park and the windbreaks of trees on the periphery of the new town. When the Torrance project ended in the midteens, there was little work in Gill's office, so Lloyd formed a landscape partnership with Paul Thiene, a colleague from the Olmsted firm. Together they designed an unbuilt resort community for Marina del Rey, California, and elegant gardens for estates in west Los Angeles, Montecito, and Pasadena. One of their major patrons at this time was the architect William Dodd, who recommended the team for a number of commissions, including the gardens of several of his clients. For the park at the

La Brea Tar Pits on a then primitive stretch of Wilshire Boulevard, Wright and Thiene created an instant Los Angeles landmark: the concrete simulacra of the prehistoric animals that once inhabited the site.

In an undated letter (c.1916), Lloyd extended a warm invitation to his father to visit him "so that I might show you what I am doing and so that we might have an outing together. I am now in shape to entertain rather than be entertained as previously. Have just become a member of the Sierra Madre Club and am slowly establishing myself in the life of this city. Have just written a little one-act sketch called 'Manikin' . . . with an opportunity for good dancing, music, and stage sets. My real work is progressing to a point where worry is finding little chance to play its part. . . . Pretty good considering that I started here without capital, name, or a very wide experience."[12]

Obviously feeling confident about himself and his future, Lloyd became even more warmly filial: "I often wish that you might be able to free yourself from the various loads you seem to enjoy piling upon your back and that we two could enter the field together as father and son. I believe we could make them all sit up and enjoy us, and we'd have a glorious time doing it. Architecture, landscape architecture, the theater, and music with the various luxuries and interesting diversions that attach thereto. And do it in a gloriously fine way too. If I only had your sincere support in the matter, I could rip the very devil out of his hole." Though the two Wrights never established a permanent partnership, they would work together on an increasingly large number of projects in the 1920s.[13]

Thiene and Wright had a close personal and professional relationship, but ultimately there was not enough work to sustain the partnership. In late 1916 Lloyd set up his own practice in downtown Los Angeles. Because commissions were still scarce, he worked for about a year as a set designer at Paramount Studios. There he did a variety of classical and medieval period pieces, lucrative work that he quickly disavowed as being "false" and "unreal." Yet the foray into Hollywood helped to confirm Lloyd's talent for theatrical effects, a penchant not absent in his later architecture.

In 1917 Lloyd met and soon married his first wife, the actress Kira Markham, whom he described to his father as "an independent. In spite of it, however, a wife. We have taken an old shack in an acre of acacia and [are] decorating the house on next to nothing. Kira is restless, ambitious and forceful, a good thing for us both. She is, however, prone to, or rather impressed by, the fact that the successful stage careers of

Perspective drawing detail, Hollyhock House, Hollywood, 1921

today (the majority of them) are made by the 'successees' selling their bodies and their souls to the 'successors.' Perhaps she'll get over it. I hope so."[14]

The next year the couple spent an idyllic six weeks with FLW in Wisconsin, en route to New York, where they lived for about a year. The move was no doubt prompted by Kira's hope for work in New York theater and by Lloyd's impatience with a slow Los Angeles practice. He had long been fascinated by the potential of air travel and found a job with Standard Aircraft in Elizabeth, New Jersey, working on designs for a new flying boat. Later the same year he worked briefly for Curtis Aircraft on Long Island, and for the architectural firm Rouse and Goldberg in New York. Also during that year the couple's theater connections led to Lloyd's designing sets for the famous Provincetown Players.

In New York Lloyd also bade farewell to his younger brother David, who was joining the American forces fighting with the Allies in Europe. In a letter to his father, Lloyd discussed the leave-taking and poignantly lamented his inability to express physically his affection for another man, even his own brother, a problem the senior Wright seems never to have had. "I felt inadequate to the occasion," LW confessed, "so long out of practice that I did not know how to meet it. He told me that he had received from you the first real letter he had ever gotten . . . and seemed much impressed, for he repeated it to me many times that day." Apparently FLW had paid David a slightly earlier farewell visit: "Sunday, the day before he sailed, you approached him and came close. I wanted to take him close but didn't know how."[15]

Lloyd then noted that even though "matters look brighter 'over there,'" he had met with the draft board to discuss his status and had "put in no claim on dependent or matrimonial grounds naturally. But the Standard people put in a claim for me declaring that I was a necessary, highly trained expert and assistant in a necessary war industry service." This rating automatically exempted him from the draft and would, he predicted, be "worth a great deal to me in a commercial sense."[16]

Although the year in New York was a diverting respite, Lloyd missed California and decided to return. His and Kira's marriage had begun to fail, perhaps for some of the reasons he mentioned to FLW, and they soon applied for a divorce. Lloyd was then admitting to an ambivalent addiction to southern California, which in 1919 was on the verge of a fabulous boom. He sensed this phenomenon and, to his credit, staked a claim to its rich potential. In those same years he would begin to build significant works of his own but would also devote much of his energy to various of his father's projects.

The first and most significant collaboration was the Hollyhock House for Aline Barnsdall, a building and an idea that would have a great impact on both of the Wrights' subsequent careers. Barnsdall, a left-wing oil heiress, was one of the senior Wright's most exotic clients. "A complex creature," he wrote of her, "neither neo, quasi, nor pseudo . . . as near American as any Indian, as developed and traveled in appreciation of the beautiful as any European. As domestic as a shooting star." Her detractors called her the "socialite socialist" and the "rich parlor communist" as she built her compound for plotting the revolution, not only in the arts but in politics as well. She later engaged Lloyd to help her mount huge billboards on the Hollywood Boulevard side of her property pleading the causes of the leftist martyrs Tom Mooney, and Sacco and Vanzetti.[17]

FLW and Barnsdall had met in Chicago in the teens via mutual theater interests, but Barnsdall, preferring the more exotic Los Angeles, decided to locate her arts complex there. The stage designer Norman Bel Geddes became her theatrical director, and Wright became her architect. Largely because of her peripatetic, restless nature, Barnsdall's theater plans went unrealized, but the house became an American masterwork.

FLW had always been drawn toward a certain cultural nationalism and, like his heroes Emerson and Whitman, to the creation of an authentic "American" culture. And his search for the roots of a distinctly American architecture led him naturally to the buildings of the first Americans: the Indians. Later he would use the tepee as a reference in the unbuilt designs he and Lloyd would do for a Lake Tahoe resort complex; but in the teens and early twenties, he seemed drawn to the pueblos of the American Southwest and their even grander Mayan predecessors in pre-Columbian Central America. As with other important influences on his art, he never publicly acknowledged the Meso-American references, though they were apparent throughout his—and Lloyd's—later work.

Built of light beige stucco on concrete foundations and a hollow tile frame, the Barnsdall house comprises four orthogonally connected wings surrounding a central courtyard. This and other walled, open spaces extend the house onto the California landscape and the vast panorama of city, mountains, and ocean. Barnsdall named it Hollyhock House after her favorite flower, which FLW articulated in the abstract cornice ornament. Could this, FLW wondered, even be called "modern" architecture? Indeed he later admitted that the California interlude was an essential respite at a time when—following the murder of his lover, Mamah Cheney, and the burning of Taliesin—he felt "on the rocks economically, publicly, emotionally." He enjoyed referring to Hollyhock as his "California Romanza, this time being frankly on holiday."[18]

Though FLW had previously referred to Los Angeles as "that desert of shallow effects," he clearly picked up on the fact that after 1910 Hollywood art directors, including one Lloyd Wright, were creating remarkable, if temporary, monuments on the southern California landscape. The greatest of these was D. W. Griffith's Babylonian palace set for *Intolerance* (1916), which survived for several years as a crumbling ruin a few blocks from Hollyhock House. Historian Neil Levine has observed that, along with the equally exotic new movie theaters and homes of the stars, "a context was established that Wright could barely ignore, especially when Nebuchadnezzar was the next-door neighbor." The Barnsdall house, "more than any serious work of architecture, speaks of the world of romance represented by Hollywood in the late teens and twenties." As such, it would also strongly affect Lloyd's architectural ideas.[19]

LW supervised the grading of the Barnsdall site, the laying of foundations and, most importantly, the planting of Olive Hill. At that point FLW sent out his Taliesin apprentice, the Austrian émigré Rudolph Schindler, who took over as construction superintendent. Although Lloyd's immersion in the project would positively affect his own emerging aesthetic of the 1920s, it would strain his relationship with Schindler, and with his father as well. The chief source of friction between the two Wrights would be FLW's inability to pay salaries and various office expenses. Lloyd kept insisting that he could barely survive without immediate remuneration. Yet, although this was partially true, LW had inherited from his father a tendency to identify as "necessities" what others would have seen as luxuries, including his club fees and the purchase of an expensive new 1920 Buick.[20]

After the completion of Hollyhock House, Lloyd worked with his father on the Doheny Ranch Resort project (1923), a luxuriant proposal for the development of land owned by the Doheny family in the then rural mountains above Beverly Hills. In several of the most appealing drawings of their lives, the Wrights designed concrete-block houses of varying types and sizes, integrated into the steep, craggy landscape with subtly positioned walls, roads, and bridges. Though it seems to

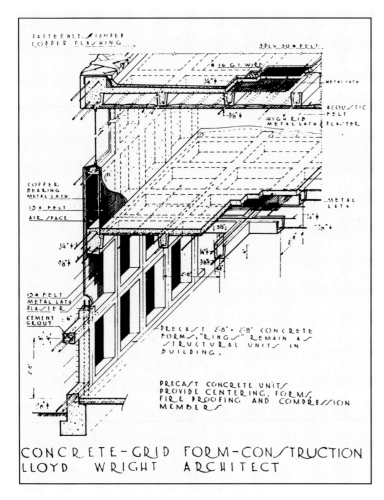

CONCRETE-GRID FORM-CONSTRUCTION
LLOYD WRIGHT ARCHITECT

Construction drawing, Samuel-Novarro House, Los Angeles, 1928

have been the most speculative and least tied to an actual commission of all of FLW's grand schemes, the ideas from the Doheny project survived as built fragments in Hollywood and Pasadena in the form of the smaller but no less exotic Mayan-inspired, concrete-block Millard, Storer, Freeman, and Ennis houses. Lloyd worked closely with FLW on the development of the concrete-block technology of these houses, having more of a role in the invention of the steel-reinforced "knit-block" system than is generally acknowledged.[21]

The tense ambivalence of his complex relationship with his father surfaced often in those years. In a particularly painful letter early in this period, Wright told his son that he was "not really reliable. You will say a thing *is* so when you only think it is so. You will promise and not keep it. You will buy when you can't pay. You will attempt anything and blame failure on others. . . . You are sentimental but not kind. You are never *poised* in action. You are quick to impute to others the quality that is rankling in your own soul. . . . You are absolutely the worst-mannered young man I know. . . . The value of a dollar is a blank to your mind. Your sense of time is loose. Your step is loose. Your grasp of your work is loose. Your sense of justice is loose. . . . Your eye is on me and my acts as you see them. . . . Turn it upon your own soul for your own good. I have been your 'excuse' for too long, my son! Too long! You will answer for your own sins. I will answer for mine. Tighten up the essential screws till they hurt. They are nearly all loose. . . . Your personal habits are not nice in spite of your manly physique and what might be good looks if you were groomed decently and were *clean*—inside and out."[22]

A subsequent letter was more conciliatory and affirmative: "Life requires technique, as does any other expression, if art. Let us learn it. In our relations as a family we have been pretty raw—savages rather. Punishment is certain and ought to be valuable. That is really all there is to a true education—profiting by the experience of joy and punishment. . . . Have a good word and a fine thought for everyone you touch. Cut out rough stuff and avoid anger as you would a house afire. . . . Pioneers—that is what we are—take pioneer's fare and no dessert."[23]

Later FLW became more paternally affectionate: "I've just come from the Storer house. It's a tragedy from my standpoint, but I can see how hard you've worked to pull it out and I approve many things you did. I have been thinking things over, and I guess in the heat and shame of the failure and loss I've been thinking more of myself than of you, more heedless than I ought to be. . . . I guess you've had about enough.

A session with old Doc [Storer] makes me realize a few things—at least you did your damnedest. Angels can do no more."[24]

The architect Bruce Goff, a great admirer of both father and son, once averred that whereas there were undoubtedly strong affinities between them, the temperamental differences and tensions had deep familial roots. "As a child," Goff observed, Lloyd "was unusually tall and soon became taller than his father, who was five feet eight inches high." Lloyd once told Goff that his father accused him of being "awkward, clumsy, and a weed." And he contended that his brother John was his "father's favorite because he too was five feet eight inches high, usually neat and handsome, and handled precious objects carefully without damaging them."[25]

Lloyd's intense relationship with FLW and his work would, with varying results, mark his own architecture as it developed in the 1920s. The handsome two-story Weber house (Los Angeles, 1921), southeast of the intersection of Wilshire and Crenshaw, reflected this indebtedness. The businessman W. J. Weber had known FLW in Chicago and had intended that he should design his Los Angeles house, but because he was impatient to get started and FLW was on an extended stay in Japan, he turned to LW instead. As his first independent building, Lloyd tellingly designed for Weber a quintessential Prairie building of dominantly horizontal lines, low-hipped roofs, and white stucco trimmed in brown that was reminiscent of numerous houses the senior Wright had built in the Chicago area in the early 1900s. Because the house also richly reflected the international vocabulary of the Arts and Crafts movement, it fit comfortably into the Los Angeles context that had welcomed the work of Charles and Henry Greene, and the ubiquitous California bungalow. Lloyd adjusted the design to the California setting by using larger windows than would have seemed feasible in Illinois and by placing more emphasis on vine-covered trellises, which connected the house to the natural landscape.

The blocky, two-story, flat-roofed Henry Bollman house (Hollywood, 1922) saw LW's first use of the "knit-block" system, in which a small air space separated double walls of four-inch-thick blocks that were tied together by steel rods. This inspired his father to adopt and further develop the knit-block system the following year for the Storer house, with Lloyd in the crucial, if vulnerable, role of supervising architect. Though the latter has a more dramatic setting in the Hollywood Hills and is more sophisticated in its layout and massing, it bears a certain resemblance to the Bollman house in the inside-outside

TOP: Weber House, Los Angeles, 1921
BOTTOM: Henry Bollman House, Los Angeles, 1922

integration of its open, second-story terraces and in aspects of its interior detailing. Yet whereas the knit-block system was the chief structural element of the Storer house, in the Bollman house it was used mainly to accent a more conventionally constructed building of wood-framed stucco.

In the same year Lloyd constructed an even more unconventional house in the Hollywood Hills for Otto Bollman, Henry's brother. He created a wildly Expressionist geometric effect by overlaying a continuous pattern of regularly spaced boards on top of roofing paper that covered both the walls and the steeply pitched roof. Other new directions were evident in the "slip-form" concrete construction of the appealingly layered Oasis Hotel (Palm Springs, 1923), the Martha Taggart house (Los Angeles, 1922), and the knit-block Millard studio and guest house (Pasadena, 1926).

The off-white stucco walls of the Taggart house were trimmed and accented with broad clusters of layered redwood planks, predicting a style that would come to be called Art Deco after its prominent display in the 1925 Paris Exhibition of Industrial and Decorative Art. The client, Martha Taggart, was the mother of the actress Helen Taggart Pole, whom Lloyd had met in Los Angeles theater circles in the early 1920s. Impressed with his ideas and talent, Helen recommended that her mother commission him to design her small house, the results of which delighted them both. Throughout the decade, the friendship between Lloyd and Helen, by then divorced from Reginald Pole, evolved into a romantic relationship, which they celebrated by marrying in 1926. From her first marriage to Pole, Helen brought a young son, Rupert, who became for Lloyd a much-appreciated stepson. In 1929 Lloyd and Helen had a son of their own, whom they named Eric Lloyd. Though Lloyd's short temper occasionally resulted in verbal abuse that he would afterward regret, he loved and took pride in both of his sons.[26]

After the Taggart and Bollman houses, LW's Deco-Expressionist penchant was best expressed in four other Los Angeles–area houses of the mid-1920s, which collectively represented the pinnacle of his life's work: the Sowden house (1926), the Samuel-Novarro house (1928), the Derby house (1926), and his own studio-house (1927). These buildings epitomized his talent for merging his own brand of Expressionism, akin to contemporary European developments, with his and his father's interest in Southwest Indian cultures as expressed in modern materials, particularly reinforced concrete. He wished, according to Gebhard, "to establish a link . . . with that which was architecturally indigenous to America. Lloyd quite openly referred to his buildings as objects which

ABOVE: Taggart House, Los Angeles, 1922. RIGHT: Otto Bollman House, Los Angeles, 1922. OPPOSITE PAGE: Millard Studio, Pasadena, 1926

Sowden House, Los Angeles, 1926

sought to convey the spirit of the American Indian." To accomplish this he chose concrete as the material that came closest "in feeling to adobe and stone and the lime cement structures erected by the Maya." The qualities that marked his Expressionist commitments stressed canted wall surfaces, oblique spatial volumes, and zigzag, chevron-shaped details.[27]

In 1926 in the Los Feliz district, near the Taggart house and his father's Ennis house, Lloyd fused those elements into an amazing residence for John Sowden, who worked with him in designing the appealingly chunky furniture. A simple rectangle of four connected wings combines privacy and openness with virtually blank outside walls, which in turn frame a lushly planted interior courtyard that brings light and air into the rooms that open onto it. The court area also served originally as a spectacular open-air theater for the screening of motion pictures and the presentation of musical and theatrical productions. The north and south wings of the rectangle house the living room and studio. Dining room, kitchen, and other service spaces share the west wing; bedrooms occupy the east wing.

The only puncture in the otherwise blank walls is the front window and entryway that opens into a cavelike stairway leading up to the living room. Clusters of concrete blocks surround the Cyclopean front portal. Gebhard observed that the blocks had a soft, malleable quality that "suggested they were made of ice cream . . . just starting to melt." In 1927 the Sowden house was considered sufficiently novel and futuristic to be featured in an issue of *Popular Mechanics* magazine. Goff admitted that it was "infinitely mysterious . . . the only house I ever wanted for myself."[28]

The Samuel-Novarro house was first commissioned by Louis Samuel, the business manager for the silent-screen star Ramon Novarro. According to Eric Wright, Samuel had met Lloyd through Novarro, who had commissioned the architect to design a Spanish Colonial house near Wilshire Boulevard—which for unexplained reasons never got built. But while the house for Samuel was under construction, the client suffered personal financial setbacks, and the wealthy Novarro came to his rescue by taking ownership of the building. There was sufficient time to make certain changes in the design, particularly in the rather elaborate landscaping in which Lloyd designed long, complexly layered pergolas that extended from the building out into the garden. Though it rears an imposing and beautifully articulated wall to the street, the house is smaller than it appears, with four vertically attenuated levels stacked into the steeply inclined hill. The only functional space at street level is the garage, with a stair leading up to the basement level with laundry, storage, and maid's rooms. This floor also contains a large space reached by separate stairs, originally referred to as the "music room."

In *California Arts and Architecture*, the critic A. B. Cutts wrote ecstatically of the music room as "the real heart and soul" of the house: "It is there that many of the great and near great of the musical world gather to hear the intimate piano and vocal concerts which make Mr. Novarro's one of the few salons in Hollywood worthy of the name. Across the floor sprawls a great polar bear rug; at one end stands the piano; and elsewhere the dull gold furniture of airplane tubing is covered, as are the walls, with a rose brocade material, the design carrying out the modernistic motif of the copper exterior trim. Adjoining is a cocktail bar with a well-worn brass rail."[29]

The main floor of the house sits atop this music salon and adjoining service area, and is attached to what amounts to a long retaining wall necessary to support the pool and gardens on the precipitously inclined slope. At the center of the main, third level are a large living room, dining room, and dining terrace to the north and a "lounge" to the south, opening directly onto the pool. Behind this lies the master bedroom, which opens to the garden. Above is a fourth studio level with glazed wings, later used as a bedroom, from which originally the Pacific Ocean could be seen. Cutts was particularly impressed with Wright's and Novarro's "unusual decor" in the dining room: "a symphony in black and silver, the aluminum legged table having an onyx glass top, the chairs' black satin seats, and the black walls being covered with strands of dull silver chain hung from the ceiling to the floor."[30]

Accenting the off-white concrete walls are highly mannered panels of hammered copper, which soon turned to a rich green. In the tall, central four-story axis of the house, this ornament gushes and then trickles from the top downward like a beautifully attenuated waterfall. The copper also articulates the contrasting horizontal thrust of the house and the pergolas as they spread across the hillside. The Samuel-Novarro house, wrote Pauline Schindler in the *Architectural Record*, "presents a thorough and sound approach to what mathematicians called 'the elegant solution,' that is, a solution stripped of the redundant, keen in the broader sense, appropriate in the exactitude of its structure." The essential fact of LW's buildings, she asserted in another article, was that they are "alive. His structures are always organisms and never a mere multiplicity of units. He has a gift for monumental majesty—which he how-

Samuel-Novarro House, Los Angeles, 1928

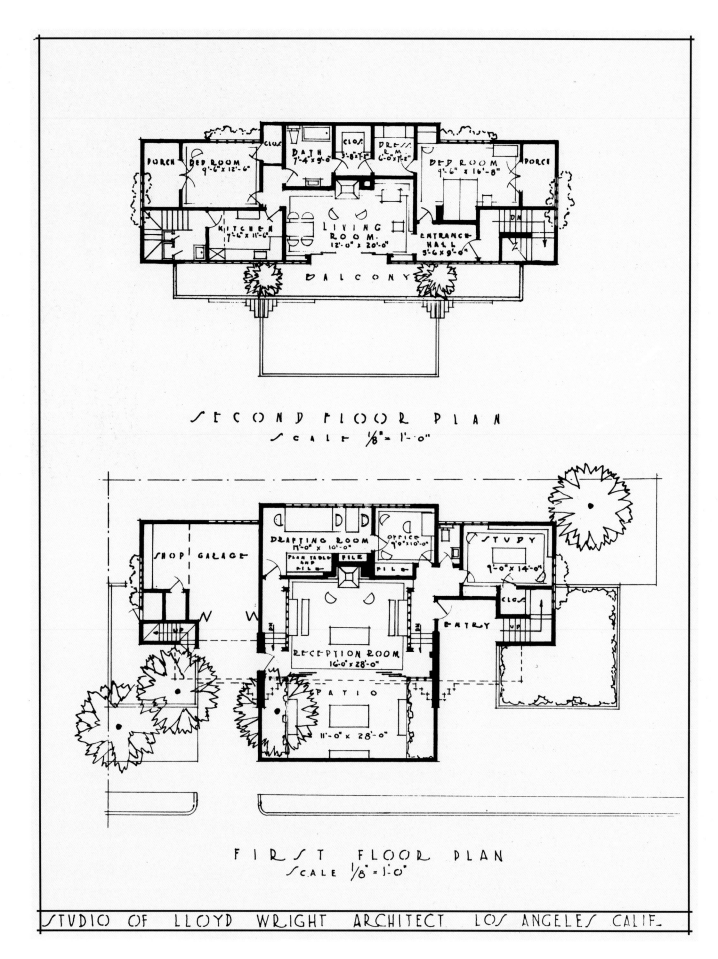

SECOND FLOOR PLAN
Scale 1/8" = 1'-0"

FIRST FLOOR PLAN
Scale 1/8" = 1'-0"

STUDIO OF LLOYD WRIGHT ARCHITECT LOS ANGELES CALIF.

ever contrasts by an abundance, a richness of applied ornament which any pure functionalist—who will naturally reject all applied decoration—will find burdensome."[31]

The powerful Derby house (Glendale, 1926) includes many of the features of Lloyd's Los Angeles Expressionist houses. Though it is less flamboyant than the Sowden and Samuel-Novarro residences, its strikingly oblique geometry makes it no less dramatic. Considerably larger than its street front suggests, its ground-floor spaces lead easily onto outside garden rooms. Upper hallways take the form of balconies overlooking the expansive living room. Though LW designed the structure to contain sections of plaster-covered, wooden stud walls, it was the closest he ever came to realizing his knit-block system as the structural basis for an entire building. As a tribute to his father he included leftover blocks from FLW's Storer and Millard houses.

Less expressively sensational than the Sowden, Samuel-Novarro, and Derby houses, the home-studio that Lloyd built for himself (1927) was perhaps his finest residential design. Its massing and its concrete-block textures suggest more affinity with the senior Wright's Los Angeles houses and the Mayan prototypes from which they both drew inspiration. More simply rectangular than the variegated, polychrome Samuel-Novarro house, the building nevertheless has spatial relationships unique in Lloyd's work.

The first thing one encounters in approaching the house, as Nin noted, is the beautifully textured front wall that encloses an unroofed patio within the courtyard. The open space adjoins the "hearth room," whose sliding partition panels can be recessed into the wall to make the covered and uncovered portions of the area merge as one. When the partition is closed, the fireplace warms a cozy, high-ceilinged room. When the space is thrown open to include the roofless patio, the hearth takes on the essence of a primeval bonfire. Lloyd placed the main entry to the right of the wall, leading into a hallway that turns left to the hearth room and behind that to the studio drafting rooms. Hallway stairs climb up to the family quarters, with the sitting room and bedrooms opening onto decks and balconies.

Of the upstairs sitting room, Nin recalled that there "was so much to see in the room that one could not become aware of it all at once. It took me all evening to absorb the pre-Columbian sculptures, the exceptionally beautiful Japanese screen, the heavy furniture designed by Lloyd. The room was full of mystery. The uneven shape, the trellised wall made of patterned blocks, the long, horizontally-shaped window, over-

ABOVE AND OPPOSITE PAGE: Lloyd Wright Studio-Residence, West Hollywood, 1927; Floor plan RIGHT: Derby House, Glendale, 1926

TOP: Yucca-Vine Market, Hollywood, 1928
BOTTOM: Carr House, Los Angeles, 1925

looking the patio below, and the old tree that, like a great umbrella, sheltered the whole house. . . . The colors were soft and blended together. The shelves held books, Japanese dishes of gray and blue with the rare fish pattern, crystal glasses, silver. Helen served a dinner lovingly and carefully prepared to blend with the place and the talk. Everything gave a feeling of luxury created by aesthetics, not by money. By work of the hands and imagination. The atmosphere was rich and deep and civilized."[32]

Concrete knit-block construction would have formed the entire structure of an unbuilt hotel and group of connected bungalows that Lloyd designed for Lake Arrowhead (1927). Strongly articulated pre-Columbian motifs characterized the stunning main building, which formed a bridge with corbeled arches over a rushing stream below. It was another of Lloyd's many great unbuilt designs.

Though not of concrete block, Lloyd's Yucca-Vine Market (Hollywood, 1928), with its canted surfaces, folding glass door-walls, and chevron tower ornament, conveyed to the commercial strip the feeling of his Expressionist houses while it predicted forms that would be developed more fully in the postwar years. A group of stores treated as a unit and oriented to drive-in traffic, the market—commissioned by the actor Raymond Griffith—was a highly aesthetic 1920s progenitor of the ubiquitous Los Angeles mini-mall of the late twentieth century. Its folding-glass door-walls and generously cantilevered roofs made it feasible to expand its services onto the outdoor parking lot. It was an Expressionist realization on the actual Los Angeles landscape of the handsome, if more rationally orthogonal, drive-in markets of Richard Neutra's visionary Rush City Reformed of the late 1920s. It also predicted Lloyd's unbuilt Drive-in Open Market and Restaurant (1931), which was designed for several planned locations, including Beverly Hills and the cities of Arcadia and Monrovia, east of Los Angeles. In a gesture that would become widespread in the 1950s, the functional, obliquely angled building was secondary in visual interest to the huge, spectacular advertising sign above it. As a cluster, Lloyd's Expressionist buildings of the 1920s comprise his strongest achievement.

For clients who resisted such avant-garde designs and asked for calmer, if nonhistoricist, reflections of the Spanish Colonial mode, LW left his artistic stamp with a mannered layering and system of proportion that recalled without mimicking the Hispanic legacy. Especially in its plain, broad surfaces, its boldly proportioned entryway, and its fetchingly corbeled central balcony, the Calori house (Glendale, 1926), constitutes a unique statement. Contrary to that house's strongly vertical, two-story attenuation, Lloyd's vaguely Hispanic Carr house (1925), spreads to the edges of its suburban property lines. Built in north-central Los Angeles, the concrete, one-story, pitched-roof residence originally featured Lloyd's enterprising use of canvas screens, which provided shade and privacy, not only as window awnings but as roofs and walls for outdoor terrace rooms.

In the early 1920s LW designed highly acclaimed Hollywood Bowl productions of *Robin Hood* and *Julius Caesar*, the latter directed by the great Gordon Craig. Then, in the late 1920s, he created two successive, acoustically successful stages for the Bowl, the first a handsome combination of stepped, Expressionist zigzags and Native American tepeelike forms. Despite its fine acoustics, however, the Bowl's major patrons disliked the appearance of the starkly angular shapes and in 1928 asked LW to redesign the structure as a shell. For this, according to Bowl historian Isabel Jones, he originated a succession of technical triumphs including "off-set rings with flat surfaces, designed with a pitch, or inclination, for reflection and distribution, and varying the angle for the height directly above the sound sources and the instrument stands."[33]

Sound traps in the rear of the ring sections eliminated unwanted reverberations. The ten-foot-long sections of the shell "were made of wood for resonance and voicing, tied together with steel rods and turnbuckles, thus putting the shell in tension as a piano sounding board." Lloyd designed the structure so that it could be disassembled and stored during the winter months or when a larger space was needed for pageants. But to avoid the small expense and effort of annual maintenance, and of disassembly and reassembly each year, the shell was left out in the winter rain and sun, and "a carefully made resonant instrument for sound reflection . . . was ruined," Jones concluded. In fact, "the shell, which could have lasted for years, was destroyed in order to build another." Designed by the Allied Architects of Los Angeles, the new shell visually was an enlargement of Lloyd's elliptical original but totally lacked its rare acoustical properties. As a result, electronic projection had to be installed for the music to be heard.[34]

In the mid-1920s Lloyd moved beyond the single-family dwelling and the larger Hollywood Bowl to the grander scale of a plan for a Los Angeles Civic Center. Various political and business leaders had proposed that imaginative architects be commissioned to create a memorable visual image of the City of the Angels in the form of a "civic center" that would also furnish much-needed operational space. Lloyd read-

TOP: Hollywood Bowl, First shell, 1927
BOTTOM: Hollywood Bowl, Second shell, 1928

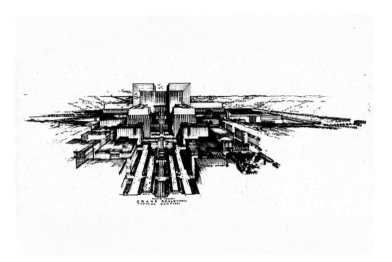

TOP: Civic Center for Los Angeles, 1925
BOTTOM: City of the Future, 1926

ily championed the idea of a plan for "the present and future development of this to be the greatest of all cities." It was something, he averred, that he had been mentally conceiving since he first moved to Los Angeles in 1913. His plan took the form of a vast urban megastructure of great height and width, anchored on downtown Bunker Hill and stretching nearly a mile from Bertram Goodhue's Public Library at Fifth and Grand on the south, to Sunset Boulevard on the north.[35]

Predicting Neutra's slightly later, more streamlined "transportation transfer" systems of his unbuilt "Rush City Reformed," Lloyd's underground nexus of transportation nodes, from rail to automotive freeway clusters, would connect via elevators to "airports" or helipads atop the various towers. With shops on the street fronts and offices high above, the center took the physical form of stepped, bilaterally symmetrical wings dominated by huge towers in LW's Deco-Expressionist style. If built, it would have been one of the world's most architecturally advanced civic centers, resembling but surpassing in size and daring the famous contemporary Oslo, Norway, city hall, which was built in the twenties and thirties. Once again, as at the Hollywood Bowl, Lloyd lost out to the Allied Architects cartel, whose resulting plan was far less progressive and memorable.

If LW's comparatively visionary civic center was planned for an actual Los Angeles site and program, his even wilder contemporary design for a highly impractical "City of the Future" called for a series of vast thousand-foot-high bronze and glass monoliths, each to house 150,000 people. In the spirit of Le Corbusier's contemporary schemes, which he would later vehemently disparage, Lloyd's towers would be separated by open spaces of parks, farms, and forests. Surrounded at the base by multilevel streets and freeways, the towers each had a bottom floor designed for commerce and industry, and higher floors reserved for residential, cultural, and recreational uses.

LW's drawings of his futuristic city contained a large element of Buck Rogers fantasy and must, on any serious level, have run counter to the agrarian/suburban commitments of his slightly less mischievous father. In June 1925, about the time Lloyd's urban schemes were presented, the senior Wright wrote him a warmly jocund letter. Though his references were not specific, he could easily have been referring to his son's hyperbolic fantasies: "I think you write well, dance divinely, and lie with charm," FLW began, "but are not convincing when you lie. No Welshman ever is. So let's go at it with the bald and naked truth and swing a wicked damn into all this shoddy and sham that passes for civilization in the E Pluribus Unum of the U.S.A. Yours, nevertheless and notwithstanding."[36]

As work slowed up in the late 1920s, Lloyd became more and more disheartened, a condition that worsened as the Depression hit and commissions became even scarcer. As always, in bad times as well as good, his closest confidante was his omnipresent father, whose own fortunes were in a similar state of decline. "Frankly, I am sick at heart and hard-pressed from every angle," LW wrote on October 26, 1929, on the eve of the fatal stock-market crash. "I have had just three dinky residences to do in the last two years, and was so poor and so poorly equipped that I could barely execute those, and now comes Helen's confinement and nothing in sight to raise a son on." Just before this, he had written and reminded FLW that he still owed him his much-needed salary on work he had done for him in Arizona. He had worked hard and given good service, he argued, "and as a reward I have been stung by you—why—you know I need badly the money I well earned . . . far worse than you do. Please send it. It is not much. That I have to beg for it is a pitiful comment upon yourself." Lloyd then softened his tone: "I'd like to have a good letter from you. You seem to be having a tough time of it. What is the matter?"[37]

FLW replied that Lloyd's "rather blue letter made me feel somewhat blue, too." The only advice he could offer was the proverbial admonition "to keep a stiff upper lip. You have real ability and enough character to make it count. Your difficulty I think is keeping cool. . . . You will get a break before very long . . . just take it easy and enjoy life a little." FLW described a recent trip to New York during which he was extravagantly honored and entertained by various luminaries, but he said nothing about paying his son the money he owed him. In a subsequent letter he inquired about his new grandson, Eric. "Make him love you and give him a chance to be himself," he urged, "and maybe you'll be better off with him someday than I am with you."[38]

Lloyd's anger at his own depressed condition was vented in those years in the form of attacks on various scapegoats. For example, in 1930 Berlin-born Kem Weber invited him to join a Los Angeles architectural association, organized chiefly for exhibition purposes, which would include such recent émigrés as Rudolph Schindler, Richard Neutra, and J. R. Davidson. Lloyd wired FLW to ask for his advice, describing these architects as "largely foreigners promoting foreign products and concepts, most of the group here not even citizens." His father's reply offered a terse reminder of American egalitarian, democratic values and revealed him at the top of his form. "There are," he told Lloyd, "no foreigners in America. Play ball."[39]

When Pauline Schindler organized an exhibition the following year of the work of those same architects and hoped to include the two Wrights, Lloyd was still skeptical, though his father was more sanguine: "I can see no particular advantage," FLW wrote, "to the father and son joining the exhibit except as the father might be proud of his son's work and be strengthened by the good qualities the son—as architect and man—might add to his own."[40]

Lloyd became even more resentful of the 1932 Museum of Modern Art exhibition, which included FLW as a kind of honorary godfather but featured the work of Gropius, Le Corbusier, Mies, Neutra, and Oud. When LW attended the show in its Los Angeles presentation, he wrote his father that it was "an excellent example of the worst of the 'Industrial Age.' Sadism cannot go much further. They can have their 'International Architecture', and I hope they are forced to live with it and in it." At about the same time, he urged that FLW "for God's sake lay off these international youths. They are just sad fools. When you get a job, hire for decent pay some American draughtsmen who can and will earn their money and mind their own business which . . . at its best, in the nature of things, is not international."[41]

Although such harangues suggested a not-so-latent xenophobia, as well as honest differences with the "foreigners" in architectural philosophy, Lloyd also could take a commendably strong stand against racism and anti-Semitism when it occasionally crossed his path. When he visited his father in 1932, for example, he was greatly impressed with FLW's plans for the incipient Taliesin Fellowship: "It is a tremendously courageous task you have undertaken," he wrote, "and everything considered, carried off splendidly. . . . Can't imagine a more interesting experience or greater opportunity for young architects at this time. . . . Hope you will not have scruples against picking and choosing certain members of your Fellowship to train as responsible aides in carrying on the routine of the place with the due preferment that additional responsibility and satisfactory exercise of it earns." He was upset, however, by the fact that Wright's Danish secretary, Karl Jensen, "dropped a few sorry words about the Jewish contingent just before I left. That is, if nothing worse, an exceedingly stupid attitude to hold. As a matter of fact . . . the best of them will be your best aides and most promising material. Let's hope the general sweep and progress of the work will wipe out that mean attitude at Taliesin."[42]

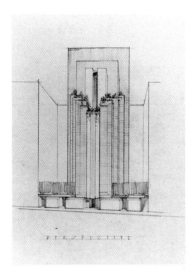

LEFT TO RIGHT: Drawing, Office Building, Hollywood, 1930;
Model, Catholic Cathedral, Los Angeles, 1931

Part of Lloyd's dejection in the early 1930s came from the effects of the Depression, which prevented the construction of two of his largest projects: a tall office building for Hollywood (1930) and a multistory cathedral tower for Los Angeles (1931). Both carried to skyscraper scale aspects of his Deco-Expressionism of the 1920s. The sixteen-story office building was an appealingly chic and functional solution that was imminently imaginable on the Los Angeles landscape. The cathedral, though far less conventional in its genre, was a twentieth-century Expressionist update of the medieval concept of the church as tower. Its four-winged floor plan formed a Greek cross. Huge concrete Latin crosses on each of the four sides overlay a fenestration grid of perforated concrete blocks tied together, as in the Samuel-Novarro house, by vertical and horizontal steel rods set in concrete. The cathedral's four connected office towers surrounded a central vertical space that extended from ground to roof. A large metal pendulum was designed to swing from the ceiling over the high altar in the center of the nave. The tower was connected to, and separated from, its four adjacent streets by lushly planted corner courtyards.

Lloyd's cathedral design was commissioned as a gift to the church by the artist Margaret Brunswig Staude, an ardent Roman Catholic who worked with Lloyd on the design of sacramental objects and various decorative interior elements. Although both the Depression and its radical design prevented the building's Los Angeles realization, the scheme was recycled and accepted, through Staude's international Catholic connections, some ten years later as the form of the new cathedral for Budapest, Hungary. "To be built in the shape of a gigantic cross," the *Los Angeles Herald-Examiner* reported, "the edifice will tower five hundred feet above a mountaintop overlooking the Danube River. Its structural theme is radically new for religious construction. . . . When completed it will cost more than one million dollars." Yet once again Lloyd fell victim to cruelly bad timing when construction in Budapest was permanently halted by the beginning of World War II.[43]

The dearth of work in the 1930s conditioned LW to accept whatever commissions he could get and to make the painful compromises necessary to keep them. A pleasant trellised bungalow for Louis Samuel (1934) was hardly recompense for the house Lloyd had built for him in the 1920s that was rescued and completed by Ramon Novarro. His remodeling of a Spanish Colonial cottage for the actress Jobyna Howland (Beverly Hills, 1934) resulted in a relatively plain, Moderne exterior that exploded on the inside with a highly active merging of LW's twenties Expressionism with a Hollywood version of the neo-Baroque. Indeed his work of the twenties and thirties seems to have appealed to Hollywood celebrities. Later owners of his contemporaneously remodeled Avery house (Beverly Hills) included the film stars Luise Rainer and Greta Garbo.

Another project, for actress Claudette Colbert (Beverly Hills, 1935), eschewed all pretense of modernist expression in a neo-Regency historicist confection. Though certain interior spaces showed LW's hand, it was the most stylistically conservative work of his career. Slightly less historicizing was the neo-Tudor remodeling of a Beverly Hills Craftsman bungalow for Alfred Newman, in which Lloyd made subversively Expressionist statements in the geometry of the roof and fenestration patterns. Two projects for the violinist Jascha Heifetz, a remodeling and a more substantial new beach house (Newport Beach, 1939), allowed LW to update his 1920s Expressionism. The same applied to his attractive remodeling of a bookstore in Beverly Hills for his friend Jake Zeitlin.

The largest, least historicist, and most significant of Lloyd's realized buildings of the 1930s was the Griffith ranch house (Woodland Hills, 1936), commissioned by Raymond Griffith, the client for the Yucca-Vine Market (1928). Along with the contemporary work of William Wurster and Harwell Harris, and the slightly later designs of Cliff May, it constituted the model for the handsome, sturdy, and ubiquitous postwar California ranch house. Because through the years it would come to seem generic, it bore fewer traces of LW's personal style than his more idiosyncratic works of the 1920s. The first of Lloyd's designs to be widely published since his canonical Expressionist buildings, the Griffith ranch house revived his talent for integrating dwelling and landscape via porches, trellises, and garden elements, features that carried over to a cluster of Griffith's nearby farm buildings. The geometrically oblique Healy house (Los Angeles, 1949) exhibited similar attributes in its sympathetic integration with the landscape.

In the late 1930s, as the Depression began to wane, Lloyd's own despair deepened. In an undated letter to FLW (c.1938), he seemed more than ever in his life to be perilously close to the end of his tether: "I remember when I was about six years old and human relationships seemed to me to be pretty mean, I told mother 'I wished God would take me back.' Now I've wished it in one way or another ever since unconsciously and consciously. Now I want to fulfill that desire by not adding any more junk to human excretions than I can help." He remarked to FLW that on his recent trip to Taliesin he had visited his mother and the

TOP: Griffith Ranch House, Woodland Hills, 1936
RIGHT: Heifetz House, Newport Beach, 1939
NEXT PAGE: Wayfarer's Chapel, Palos Verdes, 1946

THOMAS S. HINES

rest of the family in Chicago. "Mother I am concerned about. Her life is the least happy one." In looking at several decades of old family photograph albums, he was struck with the "extraordinary resemblance that all the boys have to one another, myself included. And the hangdog look that hangs over us all." He realized that in the early pictures, "we were simple fellows . . . open, honest, direct, warm-hearted as they come with a certain kind of frank courage as the family photographs show, and now we hang our heads and look out from under our brows with a surly sly look. . . . As the father of these sons, you may have noticed what I now see. If you have any photographs of them as children and as men, take a look at them."[44]

Yet within this long, painful letter, Lloyd alternated his wail of anguish with an appreciation of the American landscape and FLW's enhancement of it. The trip "brought home to me the great richness and beauty of this country and the comparatively poor part humans play in it. We have little to blame but our own cussidness [sic] and stupidity for our troubles. The hysterical human pattern will run its course but not destroy such valuable contributions to human life as have been made." In the realm of architecture, he admitted, "there is much that is valuable and that will live, and your part in it cannot, will not, be destroyed. It's too thoroly [sic] correlated with living values." After this cathartic outpouring, Lloyd concluded his letter on an almost hopeful note: "I'm back at work now. This trip has given me new courage and greater poise, and I need both."[45]

At about the same time, another undated letter to FLW expressed continuing optimism: "There is ever increasing building activity here. Looks good for several years to come. . . . If we could only live long enough, we could see and take part in great developments here. Hope we can. . . . Infinite patience is needed. Hard sledding for redheads." From the thirties through the fifties, until FLW's death in 1959, the intense, up-and-down, father–son correspondence continued. On March 7, 1941, the most poignantly paternal of FLW's letters was also the shortest. The text consisted of three words: "Dear Lloyd, How are you? Affection, Frank Lloyd Wright."[46]

In the late 1930s Lloyd took part in two federally sponsored Los Angeles housing projects, Aliso Village and Ramona Gardens, as part of a team of architects that included George Adams, Ralph Flewelling, Eugene Weston Jr., and Lewis Wilson. Like them, Lloyd was frustrated with the minimal budgets that allowed for few attempts at sophisticated architectural effects. His particular contributions were the design of trel-

lises, pergolas, and other garden elements that connected the simple buildings to the sunny, temperate climate and the verdant California landscape. Occasionally he was able, through such simple devices as craggy, variegated brick columns, to impart to the projects elements of texture that otherwise would have been absent.

In the 1940s the calamity of the war continued the deprivations of the Depression years. "The war is now taking its toll in earnest with me," he wrote FLW. "No work in sight for this year . . . and no indications that present conditions will change for the better soon."[47]

But following the war "a change for the better" finally did occur in a fabulous commission that revived Lloyd's practice, his spirits, and his professional reputation: the Swedenborgian Wayfarer's Chapel (1946–51) at Portuguese Bend on the Palos Verdes peninsula, south of Los Angeles. Lloyd designed the church to rise upon a low stone wall, with the upper sides and roof to be made completely of glass panels framed in a variety of geometric patterns. The object was to minimize the distinction between inside and out, between the chapel and the spectacular views of the seacoast and the wooded, rolling hills. While conceiving the building, LW had traveled in the redwood country of northern California and had identified with the ancient Gothic notion of a church as growing from and symbolizing a row of tall trees with the sky as the roof. Later he learned with pleasure that Emanuel Swedenborg had also used this metaphor. Lloyd planted a row of redwoods around the perimeter of the church, which decades later would almost completely cover it.

In the church's early years it received the ultimate accolade of being included in the Museum of Modern Art's exhibition and catalogue *Built in the USA: Post-War Architecture, 1952*. It also caught the imagination of the press, the public, and generations of not only wayfaring pilgrims but obsessive, camera-wielding tourists in huge, view-obscuring buses. As enlarged parking lots pushed closer and closer to the simple chapel, much of the spiritual serenity was sacrificed and the site took on aspects of a California theme park.

Yet it would remain without doubt a great work. Nin saw it as "a perfect symbol for the spirit's transparency; a perfect expression of transcendent acceptance of infinite space." Goff observed that "people feel like better people in it." He once asked FLW what he thought of it, to which he answered: "Well, the boy is getting lots of attention from it, but I don't care much for it." Goff replied, "I doubt that; I'll bet you care something for it." Wright smiled and muttered, "Perhaps . . . a little."[48]

TOP: Bowler House, Palos Verdes, 1963
BOTTOM: Karasik House, Beverly Hills, 1960

The Wayfarer's Chapel and the numerous buildings it inspired were attenuated postwar variations on aspects of LW's Expressionist structures of the 1920s. His and the era's flared, flamboyant forms resonated in such works as his Institute of Mentalphysics (Yucca Valley, California, 1946–57) and the Good Shepherd Community Church (Des Plaines, Illinois, 1957). They also found expression in such unbuilt projects as the Huntington Hartford Theater Square (Hollywood, 1950); Mount Olivet Lutheran Church (Minneapolis, 1961); and the First Christian Church (Thousand Oaks, California, 1970).

The same imagery found its way into many of LW's noted houses of the fifties and sixties, with their oblique wall angles, mannered spatial configurations, and, especially, sweeping roofs. These houses seemed to suggest a marriage of space projectiles and large, handsome insects. And they reflected similar tendencies in the late work of the senior Wright, perhaps more than did LW's great work of the twenties.

The spectacular Bowler, or Bird of Paradise, residence (Palos Verdes, 1963) could be seen as the archetype of these buildings. It bears a family resemblance to FLW's Unitarian Meeting House (Madison, Wisconsin, 1949) and to many of his late residences. It was, in fact, FLW's Hanna house (Palo Alto, 1935–37) that convinced John and Jeanne Bowler that they wanted a house "with that feeling" of integration of building and site, and communion among the house's constituent parts. Because the senior Wright was no longer living, the Bowlers turned to Lloyd, who immediately convinced them that he could give them what they wanted. The highly successful results turned sympathetic clients into lifelong champions of the architect's talents.[49]

Like the honeycombed organicism of the Hanna house, the Bowler residence is composed almost entirely of oblique angles. The house is entered from the side, off the driveway on the southeast edge of the property. A loosely defined hallway leads past wood and plastic screens, reiterating the building's geometry, into the free-flowing living and dining areas that look north across a verdant golf course to ocean beaches and the Los Angeles basin. West of the dining room are the kitchen and family room, and a wing of bedrooms that encircles the pool.

Whereas the Bowler residence is similar to FLW's Hanna house in its meandering main-floor plan, it differs in the vertically attenuated counterpoint of its master-bedroom suite. This element towers high above the main living area and gives the building its familiar identity of steeply soaring roof forms trimmed with wide, blue plastic sun screens. Similar screens adorn the lower-pitched roofs of the first-floor bedroom wing. John Bowler, a contractor, built the house and supervised the construction of the specially conceived furniture Lloyd designed for each room. The sweeping lawns are trimmed with palms, banana trees, and a profusion of bird-of-paradise plants. The latter are miniature reflections of the building's configuration, as well as the inspiration for its name.

The butterfly/spaceship character of both the Moore house (Palos Verdes, 1956) and the Lombardi house (Palos Verdes, 1965) also reflects aspects of FLW's buildings of the forties and fifties, as does the more earthbound stone and cast-concrete filigree of the Karasik house (Beverly Hills, 1960); Beverly Johnson house (Hollywood, 1963); and Erickson houses (Minneapolis, 1950).

Lloyd's defenders would argue that this work showed him as an unabashed mannerist, pushing, pulling, and breaking the "rules" of rational systems of proportion. Critics would maintain that his sense of scale was off and that his late work showed no evidence at all of a sense of proportion. Gebhard saw these houses as "agitated, flamboyant and anything but quiet. They are as assertive as a flashing billboard . . . on Sunset Strip or Ventura Boulevard. Even the California way-out designs of John Lautner, to whom Lloyd has occasionally been compared, are [by contrast] composed, calm, and in repose." In fact LW's postwar houses constituted "domestic single family equivalents to the sparkling and tinselly world of Wilshire Boulevard."[50]

Smaller, pleasant and less flamboyant houses of Lloyd's later years, such as those for the DeJonghe, Gainsburg, Honeycutt, Jester, Levand, Polster, Shulman, and David Wright families, combined the comfortably modernist elements of California Craftsman, Western Ranch House, and *Arts and Architecture* Case Study models with FLW's famous low-cost Usonian houses of the late 1930s.

"I'm finding more to do now," Lloyd wrote his father. "Have a clearer sense of the process, with a surer ability to make essential resolutions. Hard work but fascinating and stimulating and to a degree satisfying."[51] Finally, for the first time in his long career, he was getting a relatively large number of commissions, which resulted in competent, and frequently excellent, works of architecture. Still, the larger quantity of his postwar buildings lacked the taut, edgy quality of his more brilliantly original buildings of the twenties and early thirties—the apogee of his architectural achievement.

With most of the clients of the postwar years, as with those of the earlier period, LW had mixed relationships. Some adored him and accepted his proposals virtually without question; others found him so

TOP: Moore House, Palos Verdes, 1956
BOTTOM: Lombardi House, Palos Verdes, 1965

stubborn and difficult that their projected structures never reached fulfill-ment. Still others found that though he was demanding and overbear-ing, he was capable of producing buildings that made the ordeal seem worthwhile.

Lloyd was grateful to be able to share the problems and joys of design and building with his loyal and talented apprentices and staff members,[52] particularly his son and longtime associate, Eric Wright. Eric had studied with his grandfather as a gifted Taliesin apprentice from 1948–52 and from 1954–56, interrupting his studies for an army tour of duty in Korea. He joined his father's practice in 1956, became a valued associate in 1967, and continued his own practice after LW's death in 1978. Though their relationship was occasionally strained, like most such father–son personal-professional relationships, it was more consistently cordial and balanced than that of LW and FLW.

Lloyd's staff shared the keen satisfaction he took in the increased amount of work and recognition of the last decades of his life. Then, as before, he continued to express his larger ecological, environmental, and urbanistic concerns. In the 1960s and 1970s Lloyd took part in the burgeoning Los Angeles historic preservation movement, working vigor-ously and successfully to prevent the demolition of Bertram Goodhue's Los Angeles Public Library (1926) and, with less success, to save Irving Gill's Dodge house (1915). Before and after FLW's death in 1959, he consulted and worked on the restoration of the Hollyhock and Storer houses in Los Angeles, and Unity Temple in Oak Park. He also urged the successive owners of his own Sowden, Samuel-Novarro, and Derby houses, and other buildings to preserve and restore them. However, the demolition of his Yucca-Vine Market was a serious loss to the Los Angeles commercial streetscape.

Despite the substantial postwar increase in the number of build-ings he produced, he never attained the commissions his formidable tal-ent deserved, nor did he see sufficient realizations of his rich, imagina-tive designs. "If his work had been carried out," Nin observed sadly, "the world would have been dazzled by [it]. His work was on a scale which should have appealed to the spirit of grandeur in the American character, a dramatic and striking expression of a new land."[53]

After a bout with pneumonia in the early spring, Lloyd died of a heart attack on May 31, 1978. At his funeral at the Wayfarer's Chapel, Anne Baxter's reading from "Do Not Go Gentle Into That Good Night" evoked Lloyd's life experience: "Good men, the last wave by, crying how bright / Their frail deeds might have danced in a green bay, / Rage, rage against the dying of the light."

He was a tragic figure caught in the shadow of his seemingly superhuman father. Blessed and cursed by that paradoxical relation-ship, he nevertheless created, in his own long life, architectural miracles —both on paper and on the land. □

NOTES

1. The line from "Do Not Go Gentle Into That Good Night" in this and the closing paragraph is from *The Poems of Dylan Thomas* (New York: New Directions, 1971), p. 208.

2. Unpublished interview with Lloyd Wright, October 30, 1974, Eric Wright papers.

3. *The Diary of Anaïs Nin, IV, 1944–47* (San Diego and New York: Harcourt, Brace, 1971), p. 209.

4. Ibid.

5. David Gebhard and Harriette Von Breton, *Lloyd Wright, Architect: Twentieth Century Architecture in an Organic Exhibition* (Santa Barbara, Calif.: UCSB Art Galleries, 1971). The catalogue of this exhibition is to date the most substantial effort to deal with the totality of LW's achievement. Unless otherwise noted, the factual chronology of my own essay follows this indispensable document (compiled with LW's close cooperation and based on extensive interviews with him), as well as the special issue of *Space Design: A Monthly Journal of Arts and Architecture* (November 1979) dedicated to him. Except as cited otherwise, the interpretations of LW's buildings come from direct observation of them and/or visual representations.

6. Lloyd's childhood poem is enclosed in an early undated letter from LW to FLW, Frank Lloyd Wright Collection (FLWC), Getty Research Institute for the History of Art and the Humanities (GRIHAH).

7. Gebhard and Von Breton, "Interview with Lloyd Wright," June 1971, in *Lloyd Wright*, p. 12.

8. Frank Lloyd Wright, *An Autobiography* (New York: Horizon Press, 1977), p. 33.

9. LW to FLW, n.d.; LW to FLW, May 17, 1948, FLWC, GRIHAH.

10. LW to FLW, n.d., FLWC, GRIHAH.

11. Ibid.

12. LW to FLW, n.d., FLWC, GRIHAH.

13. Ibid.

14. LW to FLW, n.d., FLWC, GRIHAH.

15. LW to FLW, n.d., FLWC, GRIHAH.

16. Ibid.

17. Wright, *An Autobiography*, pp. 248–77. The most comprehensive work on this vast architectural enterprise is Kathryn Smith, *Frank Lloyd Wright, Hollyhock House and Olive Hill, Buildings and Projects for Aline Barnsdall* (New York: Rizzoli, 1992).

18. Ibid.

19. Neil Levine, *The Architecture of Frank Lloyd Wright* (Princeton, N.J.: Princeton University Press, 1996), pp. 127–28.

20. LW to FLW, n.d., FLWC, GRIHAH.

21. The most comprehensive work on this subject, which does acknowledge Lloyd's contribution, is Robert L. Sweeney, *Wright in Hollywood, Visions of a New Architecture* (New York: Architectural History Foundation, 1994).

22. FLW to LW, June 26, 1921, Lloyd Wright Papers (LWP), Special Collections, University Research Library (SCURL), UCLA.

23. FLW to LW, September 15, 1924, LWP, SCURL, UCLA.

24. FLW to LW, n.d., LWP, SCURL, UCLA.

25. Bruce Goff, "Eulogy for Lloyd Wright," in *Space Design*, p. 6.

26. Conversation with Eric Wright, Los Angeles, October 2, 1996.

27. Gebhard and Von Breton, *Lloyd Wright*, p. 32.

28. "Glass Roof Lights House Without Windows," *Popular Mechanics* (July 1927), p. 25; Goff, "Eulogy for Lloyd Wright," p. 7.

29. A. B. Cutts Jr., "The Hillside Home of Ramon Novarro," *California Arts and Architecture* (July 1933), p. 31.1

30. Ibid.

31. Pauline Gibling Schindler, "The Samuel House, Los Angeles," *Architectural Record* (June 1930), p. 529; "Modern California Architecture," *Creative Art* (February 1932), p. 113.

32. *The Diary of Anaïs Nin*, p. 209.

33. Isabel M. Jones, *The Hollywood Bowl* (New York: Schirmer, 1936), p. 124.

34. Ibid.

35. "Notable Civic Center Scheme," *Los Angeles Times*, 30 August 1925.

36. FLW to LW, June 25, 1925, FLWC, GRIHAH.

37. LW to FLW, October 26, 1929; LW to FLW, n.d. [1929], FLWC, GRIHAH.

38. FLW to LW, October 29, 1929; FLW to LW, n.d., FLWC, GRIHAH.

39. LW to FLW, June 20, 1930; FLW to LW, n.d. [1930], FLWC, GRIHAH.

40. FLW to LW, January 21, 1931, FLWC, GRIHAH.

41. LW to FLW, October 18, 1932; LW to FLW, n.d. [1932], FLWC, GRIHAH.

42. LW to FLW, n.d. [1933], FLWC, GRIHAH.

43. "LA Plan for Danube Cathedral Accepted," *Los Angeles Herald-Examiner*, 5 June 1939.

44. LW to FLW, n.d. [1938], FLWC, GRIHAH.

45. Ibid.

46. LW to FLW, n.d.; FLW to LW, March 7, 1941, FLWC, GRIHAH.

47. LW to FLW, n.d., FLWC, GRIHAH.

48. *The Diary of Anaïs Nin*, p. 210; Goff, "Eulogy for Lloyd Wright," p. 8.

49. Conversation with John Bowler and Michael Bowler, Palos Verdes, California, December 19, 1996.

50. Gebhard and Von Breton, *Lloyd Wright*, pp. 64–65.

51. LW to FLW, n.d., FLWC, GRIHAH.

52. According to Eric Wright, these included: Mike Barsocchini, Carleton Collins, Sidney Drasnin, Virginia Drasnin, Pamela Edwards Kammer, Robert Marks, John O'Neill, Peter Purins, John Reed, and William Stevenson.

53. *The Diary of Anaïs Nin*, p. 209.

□

This essay was written in summer and fall 1996 at the beginning of my year as a Getty Scholar at the Getty Research Institute for the History of Art and the Humanities (GRIHAH), Santa Monica. My debts to the officers and staff of the institute are enormous, and I thank them for supporting my larger project, *Modernism and Regionalism: A History of Modernist Los Angeles Architectural Culture, 1900–2000*, of which this is a part.

My greatest debt in the generation of the essay is to my friend and collaborator Alan Weintraub, whose commitment to the project has extended over many years. His photographs first illustrated a short essay I did on Lloyd Wright for *Architectural Digest* (May 1993), from which I have here used several selected paragraphs. The editor there who first suggested we do a piece on Wright was Lucas Dietrich, to whom we are both grateful.

It is also a pleasure to thank the southern California chapter of the Society of Architectural Historians for organizing a Lloyd Wright tour in the mid-1970s. The tour ended appropriately at LW's home-studio, where he received us before a large fire in his open hearth room. The only other time I had the opportunity to speak with Wright was in 1977 at the funeral of our mutual friend Pauline Schindler.

I am also grateful to Eric Lloyd Wright for his interest and participation in this project, and for his patience in answering numerous questions.

THE BUILDINGS

Roof detail, Bowler House, Palos Verdes, California, 1963

WEBER HOUSE

Los Angeles, 1921

The first building of Lloyd Wright's architectural career, the Weber house is in many ways an anomaly, exhibiting few of his later design tendencies. Sited in a flat area of Los Angeles, the house draws upon elements of Frank Lloyd Wright's Prairie-house idiom: low-pitched roofs, a stucco and wood-trim exterior, casement windows with art-glass mullions, a redwood trellis, sleeping porches, and a compact floor plan. The client, William Weber, president of the Weber Showcase Company, was originally from Chicago; and the commission included the design of built-in cabinetry and furniture. According to David Gebhard, Weber had commissioned Frank Lloyd Wright to design the house, but it fell to Lloyd because at the time his father was working on the Imperial Hotel in Tokyo. Several working drawings, including a site plan dated December 1920, identify Frank Lloyd Wright as architect. (Lloyd used the name Frank Lloyd Wright Jr. professionally until about 1918.) The house is incorrectly identified as an unbuilt project of the senior Wright's in the chronology of Henry-Russell Hitchcock's *In the Nature of Materials* (1942). Indeed Lloyd's father had already abandoned the Prairie vocabulary in the earlier Hollyhock House, his first house designed specifically for California. Like Frank Lloyd Wright's Stewart house (1909)—a Prairie residence transplanted to Montecito, California—the Weber house is an exception to both Wrights' notions of a California house. Lloyd would never design another Prairie house.

1 View from street **2** Elevation and floor plan, c.1921

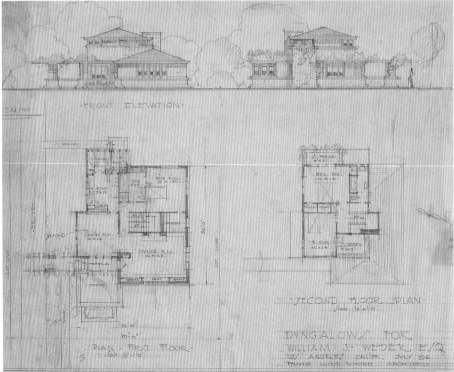

1 View toward entrance
2 Window detail
3 Exterior detail

1 Living-room alcove

2 Living room

3 Built-in furniture, dining room

4 Built-in cabinet, dining room

TAGGART HOUSE

Los Angeles, 1922

Lloyd Wright's first major architectural commission was built for the mother of his future wife, actress Helen Taggart Pole, and included landscape design. The house exemplifies Wright's flair for bold forms, textured surfaces, dramatic vertical space, and, most significant, transitional spaces that integrate house and garden. As manifest in the elaborate garden features—sunken areas with natural rockery; terraces; a waterfall; and naturalistically grouped native shrubs, trees, and flowers—Lloyd's primary occupation at the time was landscape architecture. The floor plan of the house also reveals his sensitivity to site: the building steps down the hill, with the entry on the top floor and the double-height living room below, and a bedroom suite with sleeping porch located on a split level to the west. An upper story comprises a second bedroom suite, dining room, kitchen, and maid's room and bath. Many of the rooms open out to terraces and gardens. Although the house is often interpreted as Art Deco or Expressionist, the formal vocabulary is rooted in his father's work of the 1910s and early 1920s, notably the nearby buildings for Aline Barnsdall. Striking elements include the horizontal banding, corbeled forms, geometric art-glass, and concrete ornamentation that frames the prominent window on the south elevation. Text for a real-estate notice among Lloyd's papers describes the style as "modern thruout [*sic*]. Natural characteristic colors are used, giving a quiet, rich atmosphere to a place that possesses unusual distinction."

1 South elevation **2** View toward entrance

1 South window with Griffith Park
   Observatory in background
2 Exterior, c.1924
3 Awning detail, c.1924

1 Exterior detail

2 South window, view from garden

3 Exterior detail

1 Living-room alcove

2 View of stairway from living-room alcove

3 Living room toward entrance stairs, c.1924

4 Living room, c.1924

1 Living-room detail, view from
  dining-room balcony
2 Living-room interior, south wall
3 Living-room ceiling light fixture

1 Living room from
   east terrace
2 Dining-room balcony,
   c.1924
3 Dining-room balcony
4 Living-room door
   detail, c.1924
5 Living-room door to
   east terrace

HENRY BOLLMAN HOUSE

Los Angeles, 1922

Lloyd Wright began to explore the design potential of concrete-block construction in a house for the builder Henry Bollman. Along with his own home, Bollman constructed a number of Wright's 1920s buildings, including a home for his brother Otto; the Carr and Howe houses; and the Oasis Hotel in Palm Springs, among the most structurally and architecturally inventive works of Wright's career. The structural system of the house appears to precede Frank Lloyd Wright's textile-block building system. By his own account, Lloyd introduced the use of steel rods in this house. And the house's drawings and building permit predate those of the Millard house (1923), his father's first concrete-block building in southern California. The Bollman house blocks have a hollow core with steel rods running through vertically and horizontally, whereas the structure of the Millard house lacks steel reinforcement. However, only certain walls of the Bollman house are constructed of concrete block; the rest consists of stucco infill panels on the first floor, with conventional wood-frame construction covered with stucco above. Wright later said, "Father saw it and saw that this concept could be worked into a total system, so he put me in charge of his first total-system block house, the Dr. Storer house." He also oversaw construction of the Ennis and Freeman houses, Frank Lloyd Wright's other concrete-block houses in Los Angeles. The Bollman house demonstrates Lloyd's agility in opening a house to the garden and creating a harmonious mélange of ornament. Interior designer Mimi London has since contributed her own sensibility to the house.

1 Front exterior **2** Exterior detail

1 View from street
2 Exterior detail, c.1960
3 Window block detail, c.1925

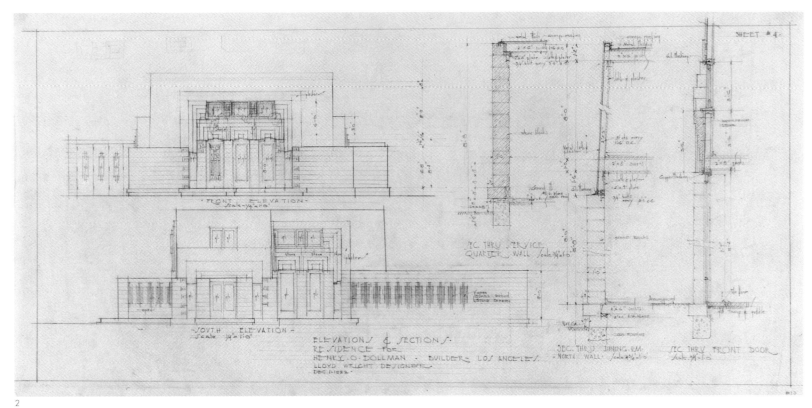

2

3

4

1 Exterior block detail

2 Elevation drawing with details, c.1922

3 Garden view, block column detail, c.1925

4 Garden view, block column detail

1 Entrance hall
2 Stair detail

1 Entrance-hall view toward
living room

2 Entrance-hall fireplace
block detail

1 Living room

2 Living-room view toward
south terrace

1 View toward
living-room alcove
2 Living-room fireplace
detail with view into
dining room
3 Dining-room detail
4 Dining-room detail

CARR HOUSE

Los Angeles, 1925

During the mid-1920s Lloyd Wright investigated the Spanish Colonial revival as an appropriate form language for southern California architecture. Both of his mentors, Irving Gill and Frank Lloyd Wright, transformed traditional building styles to develop new architectural expression. Gill's abstracted interpretation of the California mission informed much of his work at this time; the Carr house is one of the most interesting examples of this influence. Harry Carr, an editor at the *Los Angeles Times*, wrote to a friend: "This will introduce Mr. Lloyd Wright, the architect of whom I spoke to you. He does brilliant and artistic work and his houses don't look like movie sets." Unlike many of the contemporary buildings in Los Angeles, the Carr house departed from stage-set architecture through its substantial structure and plain, monolithic base. It also lacked the specific attributes of a revival style despite its ornamental grillwork and patio. Wright organized the house around the geometry of its plan. The footprint of the house fills one end of a triangular lot; the plan includes triangle-shaped rooms, with walls rotated 45 degrees from the main parti. Wright further explored flexible transitional space in the house's two outdoor living areas: a courtyard, bounded by three walls; and a portion of the front yard that became a tent room with the addition of specially designed canvas awnings. The pattern of diagonals and squares that Wright devised for the awnings echo the rotation of the plan.

1 Southwest exterior **2** South exterior toward entrance courtyard **3** View from intersection of Lowry and Rowena Streets

3

1 Entrance detail
2 View from intersection of Lowry and Rowena Streets, c.1926
3 Garage door, c.1926
4 Courtyard

1 Living-room floor detail
2 Living room toward west
  courtyard
3 Kitchen
4 Living room
5 Fireplace grate detail

3

4

5

MILLARD STUDIO

Pasadena, California, 1926

One of many opportunities that came to Wright through his father was a commission for Alice Millard, an antiquarian bookseller and client of two Frank Lloyd Wright houses: a Prairie house (1906) in Highland Park, Illinois; and La Miniatura (1923), a concrete-block house in Pasadena, California. In 1926 Millard returned to Frank Lloyd Wright to design a separate gallery for her collections, later called the Doll's House or Little Museum. After waiting three months for a response, she gave the commission to Lloyd on the condition that his father approve the final design, which he did. Wright designed a modest, rectangular stucco building that was sited adjacent to the pool and connected by a covered passageway to La Miniatura's living-room terrace. He used patterned concrete block around the doorway and windows to alleviate the studio's severe form and to harmonize with the design of the house. Construction of the Derby house was proceeding simultaneously; for both buildings Wright used perforated block as exterior screens for stuccoed wood-frame construction—a less complicated, and thereby less expensive, way to build than his father's concrete-block structures. A two-story studio space, finished with a concrete floor and concrete-block details, dominates the gallery interior. At one end are a kitchenette and sitting area with fireplace; above are a small bathroom and balcony area. Wright made minor alterations to the gallery in 1932.

1 Garden view **2** View toward southwest exterior
3 Garden view toward main house

3

2

1 View toward north exterior wall

2 Exterior block detail

3 Covered passageway from La Miniatura

3

2

1 Studio, view toward garden
2 Studio, view toward south window
3 Interior block detail
4 Interior column detail

3

4

1 Studio, view north toward balcony

2 Balcony detail

3 Fireplace alcove

4 Entrance hall

SOWDEN HOUSE

Los Angeles, 1926

In 1926 Wright's friend John Sowden, a retired painter and photographer, encouraged him to create a distinctive showplace. Sowden and his wife, Ruth, part of the Hollywood film crowd, wanted a house that would accommodate lavish parties and entertaining. Wright responded with a total environment that was permeated with a unique but indeterminate exoticism. For the house's central core he exploited the sculptural potential of steel-reinforced concrete block to produce dramatic cantilevers and intertwining vegetal forms. For the plan Wright adopted the courtyard form for a heightened sense of enclosure and privacy. Like a fortress, the house displays a nearly windowless front elevation and opens inward. Visitors began their journey below, passing through copper gates of stylized leaves and water, and ascending stairs in near darkness, before entering the inner sanctum—the central courtyard as veritable stage set. Spectacular concrete-block pylon-fountains (since removed) framed a reflecting pool and studio at one end. Sliding wooden panels perforated with a Moorish motif graced side colonnades. Yet most theatrical was the ornate curvilinear furniture that Wright designed with John Sowden: heavy couches were covered with rich velvets and finished with faceted metallic borders. The dining table and chairs were trimmed with copper ornament to match the entry gate. Ironically, Wright felt that the Sowden house, one of his best-known buildings, was "not an essential or typical expression" of his work but "a grand indulgence to the obvious pleasure of the owners." However, his father praised the house for its "treatment of the block that preserves the plastic properties of concrete as material."

1 Front exterior **2** Entrance block detail

1 Exterior at night

2 Drawing, front elevation,
  c.1926

3 Drawing, perspective,
  c.1926

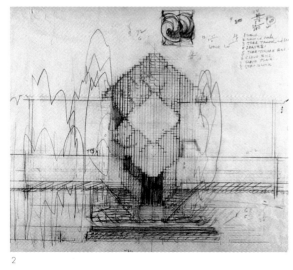

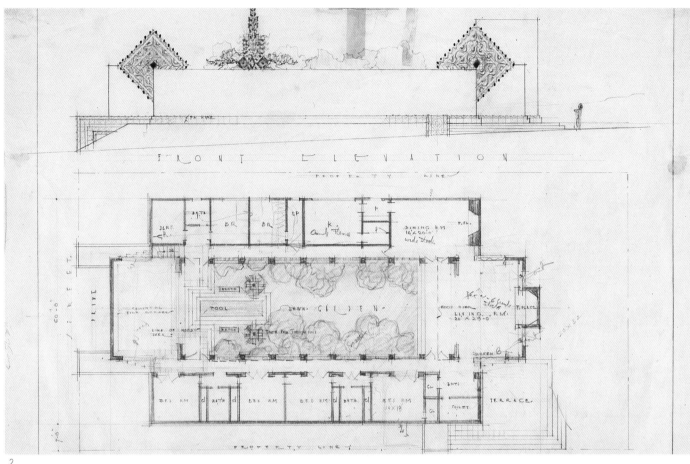

2

1 Entrance gate

2 Elevation and floor
plan drawing,
c.1926

3 Entrance gate
drawing, c.1926

4 Entrance gate,
c.1928

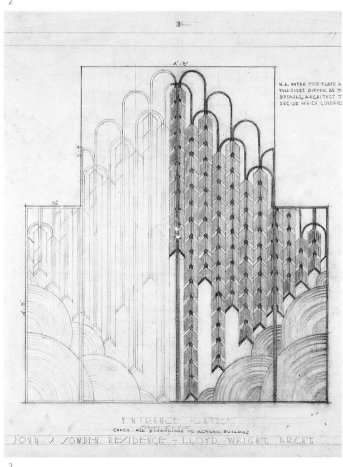

3

4

1 Interior courtyard view
toward south

2 Living room

3 Column detail drawing,
c.1926

4 Interior courtyard door,
column detail

1 Interior courtyard
with pylons, c.1928
2 Interior courtyard,
view toward north
3 Interior courtyard
drawing, c.1926
4 Pylon detail, c.1928

1 Living room, view
  toward courtyard
2 Living room, view
  toward study
3 Living-room table,
  c.1928
4 Living room, c.1928

1 Study fireplace
2 Study, c.1928
3 Study fireplace, sofa, c.1928
4 Study fireplace block detail
5 Dining room
6 Dining room, c.1928
7 Furniture detail, c.1928

1 Study, view toward
dining room
2 Honeycomb bedroom,
c.1928
3 Study bookcase detail
4 Door-wall detail
5 Bedroom, c.1928

1 Master-bathroom
  shower
2 Master-bathroom
  ceiling detail
3 Master-bathroom
  skylight
4 Master-bathroom
  mirrored door
5 Master-bathroom
  vanity detail

2

3

4

5

DERBY HOUSE

Glendale, California, 1926

Wright envisioned the John Derby residence as a house for the Southwest. Built in the new subdivision of Chevy Chase, the house deviated from the tract's prescribed Spanish Colonial and Mediterranean styles with blocklike massing that recalls both pueblo architecture and his father's Millard house (1923), and concrete-block and decorative elements that suggest the zigzag motifs in Native American textiles. Here, as in Wright's studio-residence (1927), perforated concrete-block walls form screens for windows and stairs—an early version of *brise-soleil*, or sun-break—while the overall building structure is wood-frame construction. What is particularly significant about the Derby house is the heightened spatial complexity Wright has achieved through a rotated plan and interpenetrating volumes. The plan consists of a three-story square block intersected diagonally by a rectangular wing. Wright minimized excavation into the hill by placing the living quarters above the street. The entry, accessed through a screened exterior staircase, is located two floors above street level, along with the living room and master bedroom. A balcony/loft area, which overlooks the double-height living room, is set at a diagonal to the perimetric walls. An interior set of stairs, also placed on a diagonal, leads down to the kitchen, dining room, and bedroom wing. Wright synthesized Southwest allusions with Spanish details for fixtures and interior finishes: intricate wrought-iron grillwork; dark, aged walnut woodwork; and, in the living room and dining room, walls finished in "aged gold tone."

1 Street exterior **2** View toward house from bridge

1 View from garden

2 Street exterior, c.1928

1 Entrance to dining room
2 Exterior block detail
3 View from garden
4 Window detail

1 Living room

2 Living-room detail

3 Living room, view
toward entrance

4 Living room, view
toward fireplace
and balcony,
c.1928

5 Dining-room
fireplace

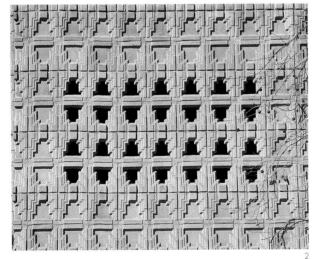

1 Dining-room window seat

2 Exterior block detail

1 Living-room ceiling,
view from balcony

2 Front exterior, detail

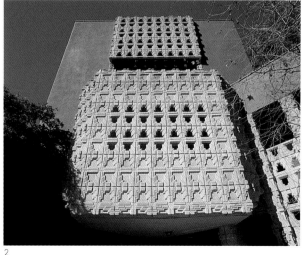

FARRELL HOUSE

Los Angeles, 1926

Much like the Carr house (1925), which is located across the street, the Farrell house exhibits Wright's unique interpretation of the Spanish Colonial revival style. His minimal approach reflects the influence of Irving Gill, which is evident in many Wright buildings and projects of the mid-1920s: the Carr, Howe (1925), Stahl (1925), Calori (1926), Oliver (1926), S. R. Smith (1926), and McDowall (1926) houses. These designs, though relatively stark, display stylistic characteristics of the Spanish Colonial revival: white plaster walls, low-pitched red-tile roofs, metal grillwork, and court-yards. For the roof of the house Lloyd specified a mix-ture of dark- and light-burned mission tile, with warped tile and seconds to suggest the patina and texture of age. He reinforced the house's Spanish flavor with a wrought-iron gate and tiled central courtyard with foun-tain. But what makes the design distinctive to Lloyd Wright are panels of concrete block incorporated into the interior and exterior walls. Included are leftover blocks from the Storer house (1923), which he had built for his father. According to Eric Lloyd Wright, it was an occasional practice of his father's to recycle materials from other jobs to enliven surfaces. But the majority of the exterior consists of bare plaster walls that act as a backdrop for the surrounding landscape. Like Gill, Wright intended that house and garden merge, so it is altogether fitting that he experimented with the mission-derived style.

1 Front exterior, view from driveway **2** Entrance-walk block detail **3** Entrance

3

2

1 Living-room window,
view toward street

2 Front exterior

1 Living room
2 Interior courtyard
3 Fireplace-mantel detail
4 Fireplace block detail
5 View toward
interior courtyard

3

4

5

WRIGHT STUDIO-RESIDENCE

West Hollywood, 1927

*There was so much to see in the room that one
could not become aware of it all at once. It took me
all evening to absorb the pre-Columbian sculptures,
the exceptionally beautiful Japanese screen, the
heavy furniture designed by Lloyd. The room was full
of mystery. The uneven shape, the trellised wall made
of patterned blocks, the long, horizontally-shaped
window, overlooking the patio below, and the old
tree that, like a great umbrella, sheltered the whole
house. . . . Everything gave a feeling of luxury
created by aesthetics, not by money. By work of the
hands and imagination.*

In her recollection of a visit to the home of Lloyd and
Helen Wright in the mid-1940s, Anaïs Nin evokes the
atmosphere of their residence on the floor above
Wright's studio. A compact building on a small corner
lot in West Hollywood, the studio-residence was a lab-
oratory for Wright's design ideas and demonstrates his
ingenuity in maximizing a sense of spaciousness, privacy, and nature. Behind the high wall along the street
is a large patio that flows into the reception area of the
studio. Here Wright received guests and clients, many
of whom still recall the scale and beauty of the space.
Of particular significance is the building's concrete-
block pattern, an interlocking mesh of textured arms
and right angles that represented "phalanxes of the
Joshua trees." This motif, which appears throughout the
house, became Wright's personal symbol. It was here
that Wright began to eliminate the boundaries
between landscape and architecture. Over time, the
building was overtaken by ivy and Italian pines.

1 Front street view, northeast corner

2 Front street view, northwest corner

1 Entrance

2 Garage

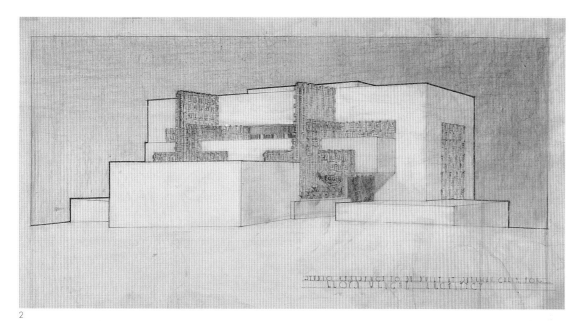

1 Exterior block detail
2 Drawing, c.1927
3 Front exterior, c.1929
4 Front exterior

1 Reception room
2 Reception room with
   Sowden chairs and
   dining table
3 Lloyd Wright chair
4 Reception room, view
   toward entrance, c.1930
5 Courtyard view toward
   reception room, c.1930

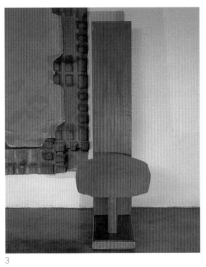

1 Living room, view west from balcony

2 Balcony, view east toward living room

3 Living room

4 Living-room fireplace, skylight

5 Living-room door to balcony

1 Bedroom

2 Living room

3 Dressing room

4 "Joshua Tree" block detail

SAMUEL-NOVARRO HOUSE

Los Angeles, 1928

When Louis Samuel, a friend from the bookseller Jake Zeitlin's social circle, commissioned Wright to design a house for a steep lot in the Hollywood Hills, the architect arrived at what he termed an "elegant solution"— in the mathematical sense. "That is, a solution stripped of the redundant," he explained to writer Pauline Schindler. For Wright the sleek, attenuated form of the four-story house was merely a response to the site—a vertical hillside skirted by a street on three sides—and structure. In a variation on the concrete-block system, steel and cement grout weave the building together using square precast hollow concrete rings, which are then covered with steel mesh and cement plaster. He placed the house's entrance at the top of the site. Inside, stairs led up to a studio or down to the main living level with a swimming pool to one side and a service area one floor below, and the garage on the ground floor. Wright insisted that the copper flashing— hammered with an arrowhead motif—be integral to the design and fully functional, protecting the porous concrete from air and moisture. In 1931 finances forced Samuel, a Hollywood business manager, to sell the house to silent-film star Ramon Novarro. Soon after Novarro asked Wright to remodel the house by creating a music room and adding a pergola and walled garden. The house suited the image of a screen idol, becoming the backdrop for articles about Novarro in the 1930s. Although Novarro left the house in the 1940s, the Hollywood glamour endures. Designer Josh Schweitzer remodeled the interior for actress Diane Keaton in the early 1990s.

1 Street view **2** Pool **3** Entrance hall

3

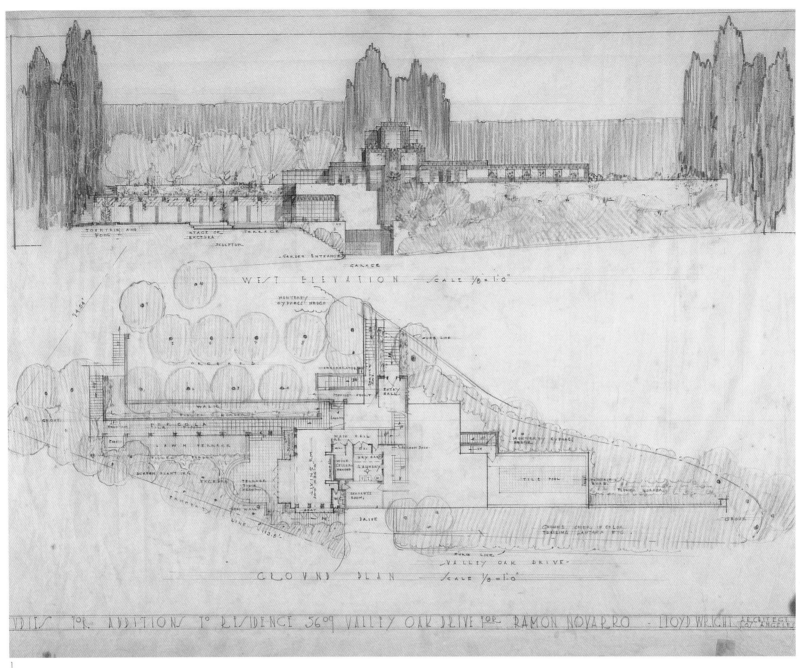

WEST ELEVATION Scale 1/8 = 1'-0"

GROUND PLAN Scale 1/8 = 1'-0"

...DII FOR ADDITIONS TO RESIDENCE 5609 VALLEY OAK DRIVE FOR RAMON NOVARRO · LLOYD WRIGHT ARCHITECT

1 Elevation, floor-plan drawing, c.1931

2 Original exterior, c.1928

1 Exterior

2 Copper-ornament detail

3 Exterior, c.1978

1

1 Garden view toward office (music room)

2 Dining terrace

3 Loggia

4 View of garden terrace

2

STUDY FOR LIVING ROOM 5609 VALLEY OAK DRIVE

3

1 View from dining terrace

2 Music-room drawing, c.1931

3 Office (music room), view
toward garden

1

2

3

4

1 Dining room, view toward living room

2 Living room, c.1930

3 View toward living room, c.1930

4 Dining room, c.1930

1 Living room
2 Living room, c.1930
3 View toward dining room, c.1930

1

1 Pool

2 Interior view toward pool

3 Fountain detail

2

3

4

5

1 Guest room

2 Guest-room
window detail

3 Hall light-fixture
detail

4 Kitchen

5 Doorknob detail

2

3

4

5

1 Master bathroom
2 Guest bathroom
3 Guest bathroom
4 Terrace, view
  toward master
  bathroom
5 Guest-bathroom
  doorknob detail

HOWLAND HOUSE

Beverly Hills, 1933–34

Wright received few commissions to construct new residences after the onset of the Depression. The commission for actress Jobyna Howland was one of his many remodels of the period. She and a number of Wright's other clients—including Charles Butterworth, Claudette Colbert, Nelson Eddy, Roger Edens, Jules Furthman, Charles Laughton, Rouben Mamoulian, Ramon Novarro, and Charles Vidor—worked in the motion-picture industry. For this project, a living-room addition, Wright transformed a Spanish-style bungalow into an elegant Moderne residence. The client's profession inspired Wright to return to the theatricality of the Sowden house. A simple front elevation incorporated ahistorical, geometric flourishes: a cantilevered cornice trimmed with dentils and windows with diamond-shaped mullions. Long stucco planes were painted with a light blue cement; the redwood trim was airbrushed with aluminum paint. Inside, Wright directed attention to the living-room fireplace, which was lit dramatically by skylights, surrounded by mirrors and glass shelves, and framed by cast stone in highly articulated aquatic forms. A journalist noted: "The sculptured salmon-colored cast stone mantel is characteristic of the architect's fresh and very personal style. An identical sense of fluidity is also evident in the plan . . . not only between main rooms, but in relation to rooms and garden courts."

1 Front exterior, remodel, c.1934 **2** Fireplace, c.1934

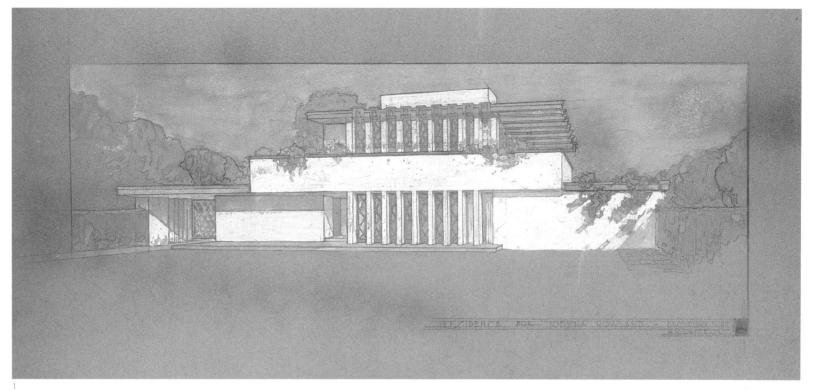

1

2

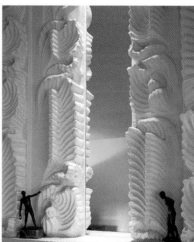

3

4

1 Drawing, c.1933
2 Fireplace
3 Fireplace detail
4 Fireplace detail

COLBERT HOUSE

Beverly Hills, 1935

Following the Depression Wright accepted several commissions that required him to work in revival styles. In those works Wright applied the essential features of the style in wryly unorthodox ways. For the residence of stage and film star Claudette Colbert, he designed a dentil molding along the cornice, applying it also in a horizontal band midway down the elevation. Colbert, who collected English furniture, later recalled: "I thought if you asked for a Georgian house, you got one. But he was devoted to the modern, like his daddy." Among the house's drawings are details for moldings, panels, and carved ornament appropriate to the neo-Georgian style. Colbert brought in designers Adrian, Billy Haines, and Hazel Ray Davis to decorate the interiors in an eclectic array of styles. In 1937 she and her husband hired the fashionable revivalist architect Wallace Neff to renovate the house. Wright could do a convincing revival, but it galled him, as he wrote to his father: "Building is booming here now but the business and profession is as tough or tougher than ever. The Colbert job has gone like all such jobs, sour with two interior decorators, three or four yes men and what have you, but I've given it a whip and now know from experience what I already knew vicariously."

1 Entrance **2** Drawing, c.1935 **3** Entrance hall

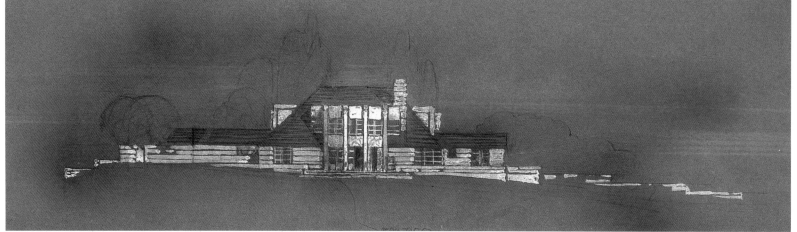

GRIFFITH RANCH HOUSE

Woodland Hills, California, 1936

The Griffith ranch house won Wright much acclaim in the architectural press for its responsiveness to site and climate. Griffith—a film actor and producer, and the client for Wright's Yucca-Vine Market (1928)—commissioned the architect to build a house and farm buildings in the San Fernando Valley. For the residence, Wright elongated the ranch-house style with extended garden walls, low-pitched roofs, and a rambling L-shaped plan. Horizontal stucco planes, redwood trellises, and local limestone further enhanced its harmonious relationship to the land. Wright integrated into the design modern approaches to zone planning and steel framing, and devised a lightweight roof with a low-cost copper-foil finish, which he later patented. The house included air-conditioning units but also featured ample overhangs and vine-covered trellises, which served as the "chief decoration." In *The Human House* (1939), Dorothy Field presents the Griffith ranch house as an exemplary zoned house in the $10,000–20,000 range. A letter from the editorial offices of *Architectural Forum* read: "In this house you seem to have conducted yourself as might be expected of the son of the father, for whose work we have great respect and which we are now publishing to an extent probably never heretofore done and in a style which I am sure will gratify you of all people." It was signed "Dad" above the title "Editor pro tem," with the postscript: "We are hoping to receive more matter from you soon. Incidentally, Howard Myers [the editor] is standing at the window smiling at this performance."

1 Front exterior **2** Entrance trellis, c.1938 **3** Rear view from pool house **4** Living room, c.1938 **5** Front exterior, c.1938

3

4

5

EVANS HOUSE

Los Angeles, 1936

By the mid-1930s Wright's clientele came predominantly from the west side of Los Angeles. Distinctive houses of this period, such as the Raymond Griffith ranch house (1936), elongated the archetypal ranch house and blended into their sites. Other concurrent works, such as the Haight house (1937) and the Avery house (1935), also reflected a tendency toward marked planar elongation. C. Warwick and Lysbeth Evans, who knew Wright from mutual interests in music and theater, were both professional musicians who, like Wright, played the cello. The first set of working drawings shows a spacious two-story residence with four bedrooms and three bathrooms. Wright tempered the house's orthogonal massing by projecting out the second floor and opening up the corners with rows of windows. He accented the spans of stucco planes with selected natural materials: a cedar-shingle roof, cypress doors and paneling, a stone chimney, stone veneer along the base, and a flagstone terrace that extended into the entry. Wright also developed a landscape design for the house with a waterfall and small pool in the front yard, and a badminton court in the back. In 1941 the Evanses asked Wright to design an addition, which enclosed part of the terrace to create a solarium with a decorative screen over the windows. After numerous alterations and changes in ownership, the house has been restored by the current owners.

1 Rear view from street below **2** View from garden

1 View from driveway
2 Rear view, c.1938

1

1 Terrace, view toward fountain
2 View from garden
3 Exterior detail
4 Door detail

1 Living room

2 Living room, c.1938

3 Fireplace detail

1 Study

2 Study fireplace detail

3 Kitchen

HEADLEY HOUSE

Hollywood, 1944

At the top of Runyon Canyon in the Hollywood Hills is a five-acre parcel of land that Huntington Hartford gave to his close friend and business advisor George Headley in the early 1940s. Within the next two years Hartford, heir to a supermarket chain, would hire both Frank Lloyd Wright and Lloyd Wright as architects to develop an exclusive resort and hotel for the canyon site. "No other subdivision of the property has been made to date," Headley wrote on a building site affidavit, "and it is my purpose to construct a residence and garage on the property I own." He hired Lloyd Wright to design a residence, a separate garage with service quarters, a stable, and landscaping for the rustic site. It appears that financial reasons compelled Headley to remove Wright from the project a year later, after completion of the construction drawings. Only the servants' quarters were eventually built—a small two-bedroom house with a pitched shake roof and rough stone masonry walls and terraces. In the mid-1960s Alan Handley, a Beverly Hills business administrator, purchased the property and brought Wright back to remodel the house. Wright and associate architect Eric Lloyd Wright designed the addition, which was completed in 1967, further integrating the house into the site by placing the new wing into the grade.

1 View from driveway **2** Carport, view toward pool
3 Exterior detail

3

1 Stairway detail

2 Roof detail

3 Front elevation drawing, c.1944

4 Exterior detail

5 Rear elevation drawing, c.1944

INSTITUTE OF MENTALPHYSICS

Joshua Tree, California, 1946–57

In 1945 Edwin Dingle approached Wright to design a City of Mentalphysics near Yucca Valley, north of Palm Springs. Dingle envisioned the city as a spiritual retreat for the Los Angeles–based religious sect, which he founded in 1927. The "science" of Mentalphysics, a method of self-realization, combines Westernized Tibetan teachings with yoga and meditation. A brochure announced the appointment of Wright as architect and engineer, identifying him as the son of the designer of the Imperial Hotel in Tokyo and stating that Frank Lloyd Wright would be advising on the project. Lloyd described the commission: "Moved by a sense of the tranquil nobility and eternal beauty of the desert, I have planned, not a city of asphalt paving and steel or of tight mechanical grid and congested living barracks, but a city of the Desert—spacious, free sweeping . . . its centuries-old Joshua Trees standing like sentinels about its homes." The compound he devised was not unlike what his father created for Taliesin West (1937–38) in Arizona. Note the battered walls, diagonal grid, and rubble-stone masonry. For the roofs Wright used tule matting, in one of the few times he was able to demonstrate the architectural application of this inexpensive material. Only a portion of the master plan was realized according to Wright's design—the administration building and caravansary (an assembly hall and hotel), and cafeteria and cottages—though he continued to work on Mentalphysics projects, including the spectacular Temple of Reverence, through the late 1950s.

1 Caravansary of Joy, aerial view from east, c.1947
2 Cafeteria brick detail

1 Cafeteria

2 Exterior detail

3 Cafeteria drawing,
c.1954

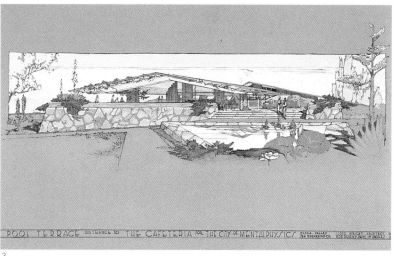

STUDY FOR THE PRECEPTORY OF LIGHT & SANCTUARY FOR THE CITY OF MENTALPHYSICS YUCCA VALLEY CALIFORNIA   LLOYD WRIGHT ARCHITECT

4

ADMINISTRATION BUILDING FOR THE CITY OF MENTALPHYSICS YUCCA VALLEY CALIF· LLOYD WRIGHT·ARCHITECT·

5

1 Caravansary of Joy

2 Friendship Hall

3 Stone-wall detail

4 Project: The Preceptory
of Light & Sanctuary,
drawing, 1957

5 Administration building
drawing, 1946

6 Project: Amphitheater
of Mentalphysics,
drawing, 1957

7 Project: Temple of
Reverence, drawing,
1957

6

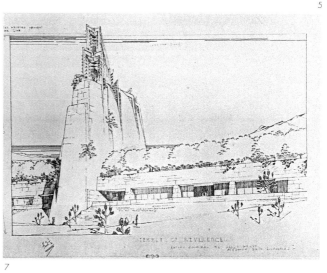

7

1 Cottage detail
2 Cottage
3 Cottage, c.1956
4 Cottage, drawing,
 c.1954

1

1 Caravansary of Joy walkway, view
   toward guest-room patio
2 Residence of Dr. Dingle, exterior detail
3 Caravansary of Joy, guest-room patio

GAINSBURG HOUSE

La Cañada, California, 1946

During 1946, while designing the Wayfarer's Chapel and the first two buildings of the Institute of Mentalphysics, Wright also worked on the design of the Gainsburg house. All of these projects have plans based on a diagonal grid, reflecting his geometrical investigations of the time. A midsize, single-story house constructed of concrete block with redwood cornices, scored concrete terraces, and a built-in barbecue, the residence is a more upscale variation of his father's Usonian house. The plan includes five bedrooms and a hexagonal living room. The design of the house and landscaping generated concern from Emanuel Gainsburg, a pharmacist, and his wife, Geneva. One early drawing elicited the following comments: "Where are the grass lawns?" "Triangle shower?" "Hall fifty-two feet long? My God." Wright also sketched a two-story alternate version, but the Gainsburgs proceeded with the single-story plan. During construction the Gainsburgs, with Wright's support, terminated the contractors, who had used Arizona sandstone instead of green copper-colored stone for the fireplaces. Like much of Lloyd Wright's work, even this modest residence received notice in the local press as being the work of Frank Lloyd Wright.

1 Entrance walkway **2** Living room

1 View toward barbecue
   area
2 View of terrace and pool
3 Rear view from garden,
   c.1950

SWEDENBORGIAN CHAPEL
(WAYFARER'S CHAPEL)

Palos Verdes, California, 1946–51

The one building that radically altered Wright's low profile and brought him (and on occasion, his father) national attention was the Swedenborgian Chapel, known as the Wayfarer's Chapel, which began construction in 1949. Commissioned by the Swedenborgian Church of the New Jerusalem at Portuguese Bend in Rancho Palos Verdes, it attracted the notice of architecture critics and travel editors, among many others. Wright was subsequently considered for various church commissions through the 1960s. The Wayfarer's Chapel is the fullest expression of Wright's propensity to integrate architecture with landscape. The redwood structure—Y-shaped frames supporting large panels of glass—is clearly articulated. Throughout the plan and elevation are 30-60-90–degree triangles, a symbolic reference to the triad and a means of making the glass enclosure as inconspicuous as possible. The ceiling alternates triangular panels of glass and blue tile to provide views of the sky and mountains. Berms of native stone set in concrete with steel reinforcement echo his father's desert rubble-stone construction at Taliesin West and serve as walls, foundations, and planters for a lush landscape of ferns and coastal redwoods. Wright intended that the redwoods surround and fully shade the building to create a "tree chapel." "I wanted particularly to allow those trees and those trunks to be seen, and the space beyond and into infinity to be observed, to create this sense of outer as well as inner space," he stated. For Wright, the trees provided a heightened sense of shelter and living space: "The concept was for life—infinite life, infinite space."

1 Chapel exterior, c.1958 **2** Chapel interior
3 View toward chapel entrance

3

2

3

4

1 Chapel and tower from garden
2 Aerial view of chapel, c.1958
3 Chapel, drawing, c.1954
4 Lloyd Wright at chapel, c.1976
5 Chapel, drawing, c.1947

5

JESTER HOUSE

Palos Verdes, California, 1949

In 1949 Wright designed a house for Ralph Jester, a longtime friend and previous client of his father's. (The 1938 Jester house, also planned for Palos Verdes, is Frank Lloyd Wright's first project to employ a circular design unit. The design was finally built in 1971, with some variations, at Taliesin West.) Lloyd Wright and Jester met through Wright's aunt Maginel and shared interests in architecture and film. Jester, a multitalented artist, came to California to work with director Cecil B. DeMille as a costume designer at Paramount Studios. Among his credits are the films *The Crusades* (1935), *The Buccaneer* (1938), and *The Ten Commandments* (1956). Well connected in Hollywood and Palos Verdes, Jester introduced Wright to future clients— Elizabeth Schellenberg and Narcissa Cox Vanderlip, the principal patrons of the Wayfarer's Chapel; and actress Claudette Colbert—and Wright thanked his friend by naming him associate architect on the drawings for both projects. Working closely with Jester, Wright devised a modest house with a 60-degree parallelogram module, concrete-block details, built-in furnishings, and optimal views of the cove and bluff below. Given the involvement of two strong personalities, the design process was not always smooth, according to Ralph's wife, Lois. At one point construction was delayed so that Wright could review masonry samples on-site, but the coursing pattern finally was selected without him—and Wright was furious. Lois recalls that years later, when Wright paid a visit, he said: "You know, I had forgotten what a beautiful house I designed for you." And so it was a happy ending in every respect.

1 View from garden 2 Master-bedroom terrace 3 Living room
4 Dressing room 5 Brick detail 6 Exterior, c. 1952

3

4

5

6

DORLAND HOUSE

Altadena, California, 1949

Wright designed both the Lubsen (1940) and Dorland houses as low-cost houses of quality. These modest Altadena residences may be interpreted as extensions of Frank Lloyd Wright's concept of the Usonian house, a prototype for compact, affordable single-family housing. The construction date of the Sturges house (1939), his father's first Usonian house in southern California, coincides with Lloyd's initial efforts in this area. Wright described the Lubsen house as a "California residence for typical small family," with "typical elements of 'the house of tomorrow.'" It was during a visit to the Lubsen house that Dorland, an assistant principal at Los Angeles Junior High School, and his wife learned about Wright. The Dorland house employed characteristic elements of the Usonian house: a low budget ($6,000 to $7,000), a living room with dining alcove, a concrete slab floor, and a carport. Unlike the rough board-and-batten walls of the Lubsen house, those of the Dorland house were constructed of concrete block, as requested by the clients. The plan, based on a 3-foot-square module, comprised one bedroom and bathroom, with a screened porch that Wright later converted with an addition (now removed) into two bedrooms for their son and daughter. Wright also designed the swimming pool and several pieces of furniture, including a dining and three end tables. In 1950 Dorland wrote to Wright: "We have been in your beautiful house nearly seven weeks and are still finding new and interesting views. It isn't like living, it's like being on a vacation."

1 View from pool **2** Exterior detail **3** View from street

3

RESIDENCE FOR MR. & MRS. ALLEN DORLAND PASADENA CALIF LLOYD WRIGHT ARCHITECT

1 Drawing, c.1949
2 Exterior
3 Front exterior, c.1951

1 Living room,
  view toward
  bedroom wing
2 Kitchen detail
3 Furniture detail
4 View toward
  entrance

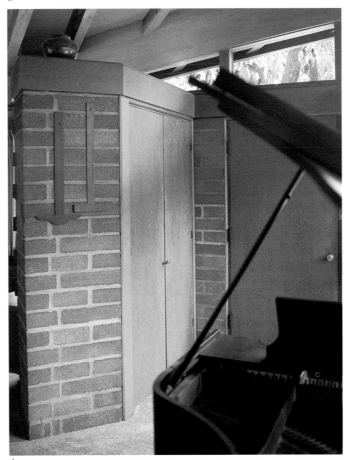

NEWMAN HOUSE

Pacific Palisades, California, 1949–52

In 1948 Lloyd Wright's friends Martha and Alfred Newman asked him to design them a new house in Pacific Palisades. Alfred Newman, the noted film composer, and Wright shared a passion for music, and Wright often attended chamber music "fests" at the Newmans' home. Wright attracted other clients who were prominent in the music world, including Jascha Heifetz, Louis Kaufman, Gregor Piatigorsky, Lawrence Tibbett, and C. Warwick and Lysbeth Evans. This commission marked his second for Newman: In 1934 Wright remodeled his Craftsman bungalow in Beverly Hills into a half-timbered English cottage. For the new home, the Newmans imagined a ranch house that was "rugged . . . in the sense of perhaps some brick facing." And they wanted a "sense of security, warmth and snugness, completely without austerity, but certainly not without dignity." Wright responded with a two-story wood-frame and stucco house topped by a pitched roof with a cruciform antenna at one end. The main block was flanked by detached wings separated by breezeways; and brick was used for the chimney, interior finishes, terraces, and garden walls. Wright designed the living room specifically for chamber music, with a free-flowing plan, a great beamed ceiling, and ample space for the family's piano and other instruments. The openness of the plan derived from the use of a 60-120–degree parallelogram module. The commission included landscape design as well as furniture for the living and dining rooms—all based on the hexagon—and, of course, music stands.

1 View from driveway **2** Wine-cellar door detail **3** View from pool **4** Exterior view, c.1955 **5** Drawing, c.1950

3

4

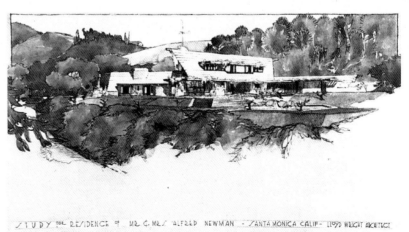

5

1 Bar, living room
2 Breakfast room
3 Furniture detail
4 Living room, drawing,
   c.1950

PROPOSED LIVING ROOM FOR MR&MRS ALFRED NEWMAN · LLOYD WRIGHT ARCHT

ARTHUR ERICKSON HOUSE

Edina, Minnesota, 1950

Arthur and Alfred Erickson both admired the Bel Air residence that Wright built for their friend P. J. Healy in 1949. The two ran Erickson Brothers, a petroleum business in Minneapolis. They soon commissioned Wright to design them each a house in the neighborhood of Edina, Minnesota. Two of the architect's few built works outside of California, the Erickson houses—like the Healy house—were low-slung, single-story ranch houses with customized features. Though they shared the same building specifications, plan module, and palette of materials, the houses were created to suit the specific needs of each brother. In 1951 Arthur, who worked most closely with Wright, asked him to redesign one feature in his house, noting that "the design for this screening . . . is so outstanding its use in both homes poses a problem" because it would be "readily recognizable as having been used in both homes." He added: "The similarity of construction that has been used in our homes has proven to be very advantageous, and aside from this one matter of screening has been enough dissimilar so as not to be at all noticeable." Wright readily complied with the request, and also designed for Arthur a music cabinet, high stool, and coffee table in the 60-120–degree parallelogram module to complement the house. The Erickson houses led to other commissions for Wright: a house that was designed and built for Arthur's daughter and son-in-law Charles Pihl (1961) in Minnetonka, Minnesota; the Holiday Bargain Fair and Service Station for Erickson Petroleum Corporation (1964), and the Erickson Memorial Garden (1965), two projects designed for Minneapolis.

1 View from street
2 Bedroom wing
3 View from lawn
4 Drawing, c.1950

3

4

1

1 Master-bedroom terrace

2 Terrace planter

1 Window detail
2 Construction
  photograph,
  c.1951
3 Roof detail

1

2

3

4

1 Bedroom-wing hallway

2 Column detail

3 Bedroom glass wall

4 Light fixture

5 Entrance area

6 Living room

7 Liivng-room screen

8 Screen detail

5

6

7

8

SHULMAN HOUSE

Los Angeles, 1950

At the beginning of the 1950s, Wright's office was filled with work. Among the jobs then in process or in construction were the Wayfarer's Chapel, a studio addition for Jascha Heifetz, a half-dozen houses in southern California and two in Minnesota. Whenever possible, Wright supervised construction and even reduced his supervision fees to ensure satisfactory results, as he did for the Shulman house. The Shulmans gave Wright a detailed list of requirements for their three-bedroom, two-bath home, the final one being "a hell of a lot for what we want to spend." Wright incorporated most of their wishes in a 120-degree L-shaped plan based on a diagonal module, which placed the main living spaces on one floor. At one end a living-room balcony, paneled in lapped plywood, cantilevers over the pool area below. To lower the budget, Shulman asked Wright to scale down the initial scheme; but during construction he requested and received sketches for a bedroom addition. Two weeks later Shulman terminated the architect's services without paying for supervision. Wright fired back: "Now, you full well know that the task of following through the slow processes of a novice in construction work can only be excessively expensive to an architect." Shulman countered that the supervision was inadequate and threatened to warn other "wide eyed 'novices,'" stating that "this building may represent a wonderful architectural monument for you but it represents a financial mausoleum for me." Wright did not complete the house; subsequent owners have made substantial additions and alterations.

1 View from driveway **2** Roof detail

1 View from pool, remodel

2 View from pool, 1990

3 Entrance hall

4 Stairs from pool area to entrance hall

KROPP HOUSE

Chardon Farms, Grayslake, Illinois, 1952

Following his first visit to Chardon Farms, Wright wrote with enthusiasm to the Kropps about the opportunity presented by their residential commission, noting especially the setting: "The countryside is beautiful—I was impressed with its similarity to the Kentucky bluegrass country." To tailor the house to its site on a hill, Wright employed native materials and agrarian iconography, as well as forced air-conditioning and radiant heating that would allow the house to be opened to the outdoors—even in cool weather. Roy Kropp, who ran Kropp Forge Co. in Chicago, and his wife were friends with two other Chicago industrialists who commissioned works in southern California by the Los Angeles–based architect: P. J. Healy of Arrow Petroleum and Frank O. Howard of the Howard Foundry Company. The Kropps greatly admired the Healy house and asked Wright for a sketch of its doorway glass design. But Wright of course proposed to create a glass design specifically for their entrance. Like the Healy house, the Kropp house is a sprawling ranch-style residence with Arizona flagstone terraces, sand-blasted glass details, and a plan based on a 60-120–degree diagonal grid. However, the house's extensive plan and myriad details—a log room with a chimney of native stone, a wooden screen with a snowflake pattern in the daughter's room, and a "sleeve" to enable an existing tree to become part of the building —mark it among the most palatial of Wright's built residences.

1 Exterior **2** Roof detail **3** Entrance courtyard **4** View toward master-bedroom balcony **5** Drawing, c.1952

4

5

1 Pool-area detail

2 View toward pool area

3 View through enclosed
fountain to pool

1

2

4

5

1 Television antenna

2 Chimney

3 Column detail

4 Detail of Chardon Farms motif

5 View toward entrance courtyard

1 Living room

2 Stairway

3 Bedroom-wing gallery

4 View toward living room

5 Living room

2

3

4

5

1 Bar, family room

2 Guest bedroom

3 Guest dressing room

4 Shooting gallery

5 Family room

MOORE HOUSE

Palos Verdes, California, 1956

The well-publicized success of the Wayfarer's Chapel generated a number of residential commissions in the Palos Verdes area, four of which were built: the Jester house (1949), the Moore house (1956), the Bowler house (1963), and the Lombardi house (1965). The Moores were already living on the peninsula but decided they needed more space for a growing family. According to Louis Moore, it was his wife Marriott's interest in modern architecture that impelled them to hire Wright. Foremost in their wishes was a house that would take advantage of the ocean view. To this end Wright elevated the common areas—the living room, dining room, and kitchen—to the second floor and placed all the bedrooms (except for the master bedroom) downstairs. A boomerang-shaped plan maximized views along the west, ocean-facing elevation, and a second-story terrace wrapped around the front. For the main living area, Wright provided unobstructed vistas of the bay through the use of mitered glass corners, and a structural wood ring devised by Wright associate Bob Marks eliminated the need for crossbeams. The Palos Verdes Art Jury, which favored Mediterranean-style houses, objected to the use of Palos Verdes stone, the extended roof overhangs, and the house's unusual appearance, which some still liken to a spaceship. But eventually Wright prevailed, and the house was approved. Louis later recalled driving around the neighborhood to show the architect the lot he had purchased, pointing to a nearby home, and saying, "Mr. Wright, I don't want a big, square house like that one." Wright replied, with a grin, "Sir, you insult me."

1 Exterior **2** View from balcony **3** View from street
4 Drawing, c.1956

3

4

RESIDENCE FOR DOCTOR & MRS. LOUIS T. MOORE PALOS VERDE ESTATES CALIF LLOYD WRIGHT ARCHITECT

1

2

1 Roof and balcony detail
2 Roof detail

1 Stone detail

2 Dining-room screen detail

3 View of rear stairway

4 Living room

LEVAND HOUSE

Beverly Hills, 1958

The Levand house and carport embodies the direction of Wright's design tendencies at the end of the 1950s. In this elegant Trousdale Estates residence for a real-estate broker, Wright explored the expressive potential of concrete block and incorporated gold anodized-aluminum fasciae, trim, and finishes throughout the house. He specified that the roofing be sprayed with a light coating of bronze or aluminum gold powder to match and designed a bowl edged with a stylized golden monograph. Wright even experimented with mixing gold anodized-aluminum dust into concrete for an interior floor finish. The focus of the spacious open plan, built on a 4-foot-square module placed on point, was a large reception area with two fireplaces. Wright integrated into the house up-to-date domestic technologies, including built-in stereophonic speaker outlets, a revolving television, and synthetic finishes. For the entry he designed a plastic-covered trellis, later deemed unworkable and prohibitively expensive by the owner. Among the building's features characteristic of Wright were extended cantilevered roofs; indoor-outdoor living spaces, including a solarium; and a radiant heating system. However, the most outstanding attribute of the house was its landscaping: vertical and hanging gardens, and a spectacular cascading fountain designed to flow down from the hill at the north end of the site to the swimming pool to the south. In a perspective drawing of the house rendered in gold, Wright captures an evanescent quality evocative of Japanese scroll paintings.

1 Entrance **2** View from pool **3** Drawing, c.1958

1 View toward pool terrace

2 Screen detail

3 View toward entrance courtyard

DEJONGHE HOUSE

Los Angeles, 1959

The DeJonghe house provides an interesting case study in which to analyze the continued influence of the architecture of Frank Lloyd Wright on that of his son. The two-tiered stone arcade of the house is unique in Lloyd Wright's oeuvre. The house's formal vocabulary —rough-hewn stonework and a jagged roofline of staggered wood beams—is also unusual, suggesting an amalgamation of ideas. Mabel DeJonghe later recalled that the concept was to set the house into the hill of its rustic site in the Wonderland section of the Hollywood Hills. But its front elevation also brings to mind the arches of Roman aqueducts and his father's design for the Marin Civic Center (1957). Daniel DeJonghe came from Holland, where he had learned about Frank Lloyd Wright, and promised himself that if he built a house Wright would design it. The DeJonghes first approached Lloyd Wright in 1949, but design work did not begin until 1959, the year the senior Wright died. The initial design was based on a sketch by Daniel of a floor plan for a modest two-bedroom, single-story residence. Construction finally began in 1962, but was besieged by delays and lawsuits as the DeJonghes struggled with an incompetent contractor. In the midst of legal battles, Daniel wrote, "We had Wright design it, we set out with Wright, and we are going to finish this with Wright or we will not finish at all." The present owner, an architect, has restored and renovated the house.

1 Roof detail **2** View from bedroom terrace
3 View from street

3

1 View of bedroom
wing from east
2 Drawing, c.1959
3 Exterior detail
4 Hallway, view
toward entrance

RESIDENCE FOR MR. & MRS. DANIEL DE JONGHE · 9020 CRESCENT DRIVE · LOS ANGELES, CALIF. · LLOYD WRIGHT · ARCHITECT

2

3

4

1 East exterior

2 Living room

3 Living-room exterior at night

4 Dining-room window detail

3

4

2

2

3

4

5

1 Living-room–dining-room lighting detail

2 Original kitchen detail, 1989

3 Kitchen screen detail, 1989

4 Kitchen screen detail

5 Kitchen

KARASIK HOUSE

Beverly Hills, 1960

The Karasiks were looking for an architect to design a house for their narrow, sloping lot in Beverly Hills when they were referred to Lloyd Wright. Sofia Karasik, originally from Mexico, had never heard of him or even his father, but Jacob, a builder by profession, certainly had. After a meeting at the Doheny office, they hired Wright in 1959. The Karasiks, who had four children, asked for a separate area for Jacob's office and a special place for music and entertaining. It was especially important that all the main living spaces be placed on one floor (a previous architect had designed a four-level house for the steep site). Wright's two-story plan fulfilled all these requirements. All the principal rooms are located on the top, main level. Wright sited the living room for maximum views of the adjacent park and designed a special niche for the piano. A courtyard is at the heart of the house, which recalls the plans of both the Sowden and Hollyhock houses. However, in this case it is fully open to the garden one level below, with stairs that lead down to the barbecue area and swimming pool. Jacob's office, which has its own separate entry, is also on the lower level. Construction, which lasted four years, was complicated by major excavation and many customized features: steel-reinforced concrete grillwork, plastic roofing, plastic soffits, and built-in furniture. Although the Karasiks chose most of the colors and finishes for the house—Honduras walnut paneling, terrazzo floors, and bleached mahogany furniture—Wright selected Formica for the master bathroom in his favorite color: lavender.

1 View from pool **2** Pool area, column detail

1 View from street

2 Drawing, c.1960

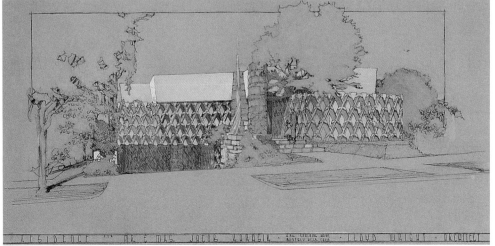

2

3

1 Masonry detail

2 Entrance hall,
view toward
courtyard

3 Stairs down to
courtyard

4 Living-room
fireplace detail

5 Courtyard, view
of stairs leading
up to main floor

4

5

1

2

3

4

1 Entrance-hall detail
2 Interior detail
3 Entrance hall
4 Master bathroom

1 Family room, fireplace, bar

2 Living-room–dining-room divider

3 Dining room

BOWLER HOUSE

Palos Verdes, California, 1963

While searching for an architect to design their house in Palos Verdes, Jeanne and John Bowler came across photographs of Frank Lloyd Wright's Hanna house (1935–37) in a design magazine. The indoor-outdoor spaces and the openness of the plan, based on a hexagonal module, appealed to them. In fact it was the only house they could agree upon. Soon after they were surprised to discover a listing for a "Lloyd Wright" in the phone book. They contacted him and asked if he could design a house with the same feel as the Hanna house. Wright said that he could; he had even worked on the original. With this one mandate, the Bowlers otherwise gave him complete freedom. The result was the Bird of Paradise house—a name that reflects its steeply pitched roof. Wright used a triangular module to create spacial flow like that of the Hanna house, but the house's distinct character derived from the program, site, and materials. It was built of concrete and Santa Maria stone, with blue corrugated fiberglass along the pitched roof and exterior balustrade to intensify the color of the sky and heighten a sense of shelter. Wright even designed angled furniture for the living and dining rooms. Although the entire project exceeded their budget, John Bowler, an industrial building contractor, built the house over four years. (Eric Lloyd Wright oversaw renovations of the house in 1991.) In one of few design changes, the Bowlers modified a freestanding cabinet in the prismatic master bathroom, finishing it with mirrors instead of Formica. Wright, whose exacting nature is well known, first saw the result with his friend the architect Bruce Goff. Both of them were surprised—and delighted.

1 Exterior detail **2** Balcony detail

1 View from front lawn
2 Aerial view, c.1967

1 Pool
2 View from pool, c.1968
3 Drawing, c.1963
4 Roof detail
5 Entrance, c.1968
6 Entrance

RESIDENCE FOR MR. & MRS. JOHN P. BOWLER PALOS VERDES CALIFORNIA · LLOYD WRIGHT · ARCHITECT 858 N. DOHENY DRIVE LOS ANGELES CALIF · JUNE 1963

3

4

5

6

1 Column
detail
2 Dining
room

2

1 View toward
living-room fireplace
2 Living room
3 Dining room, c.1968
4 Dining-room window
detail

1 Sitting area

2 Master bedroom

3 Sitting area, view toward
master bedroom, c.1968

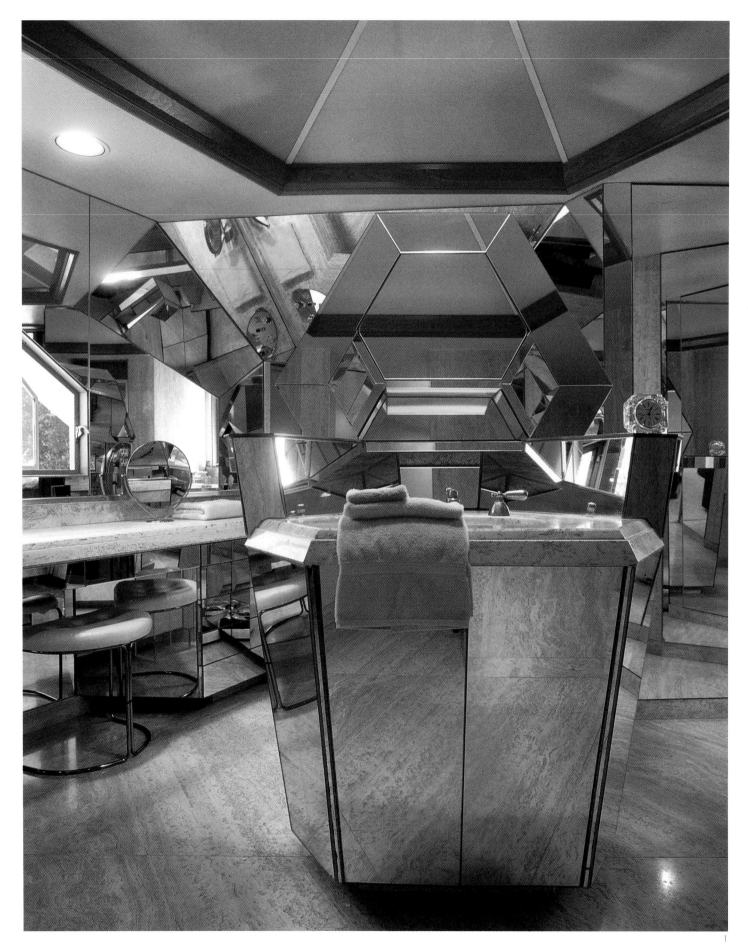

1

1 Master bathroom
2 Master-bathroom mirror detail
3 Master-bathroom vanity detail
4 Master-bathroom mirror detail

JOHNSON HOUSE

Hollywood, 1963

When Beverly Edna Johnson met Wright while writing a feature on the architect for the *Los Angeles Times*, she was impressed by the spaciousness of his studio and its walled garden: "It was just so breathtaking, and I decided that if I built a house, I would have him design it. Why not get the best?" In 1963 she commissioned a house to share with her mother for a steep fan-shaped lot large enough to also accommodate a corral for her horses. It was Wright's concept for the house to span across the canyon at the bottom of the site. For views and privacy, the main living spaces were on the second floor and the house appeared closed to the street, opening instead to the back terraces and gardens that Wright also designed. Johnson specifically requested the use of concrete-block ornament, prompting Wright's first use of the material since the 1920s (although cast-stone screen units appear in the 1960 Karasik house). For the block motif, Wright abstracted the pine tree: chevrons represent needles and multifaceted squares on point, pinecones. The budget limited the use of concrete blocks to exterior screens, fireplace ornament in the living room, a light pylon, and a mailbox. The house reflects Wright's distinctive sense of color: the exterior was lavender, with brown-green accents. In the living room Wright juxtaposed violet and chartreuse with red-tinted plaster, a color requested by the client. Eric Lloyd Wright, who served as associate architect on the house, designed and built a swimming pool and pool-house addition in 1993.

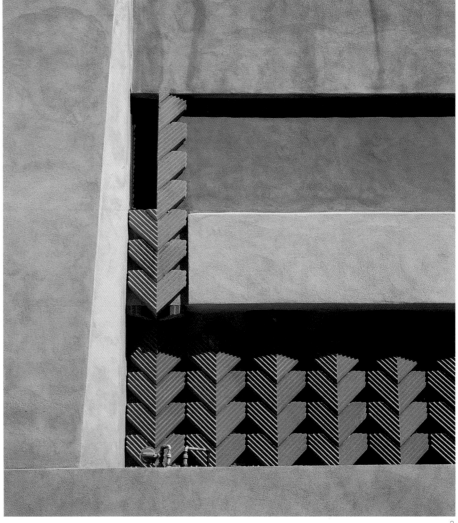

1 View from west **2** Exterior detail

1 View from street

2 Drawing, c. 1963

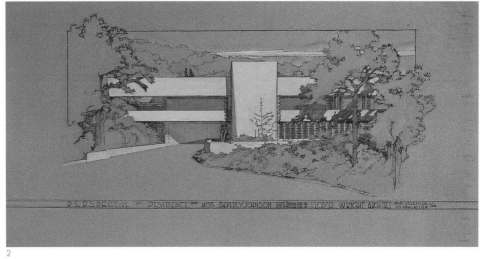

1 View from pool-house

2 Ornament detail

3 Pool-house addition by Eric Lloyd Wright

1 Terrace, view toward living room

2 Terrace

3 Living room

1 Dining room
2 Master bedroom,
 view toward terrace
3 Den
4 Kitchen
5 Living-room fireplace

2

4

5

LOMBARDI HOUSE

Palos Verdes, California, 1965

After interviewing one architect to design a residence for their hillside lot, the Lombardis considered calling Wright but assumed that the architect of the Wayfarer's Chapel would be too expensive. They inquired anyway and discovered how reasonable his fees were: 10% of construction costs (less than the other architect). Wright met them at the site and developed a plan to realize the wishes of the couple and their five children: a view from every room, a separate bedroom wing for the daughters, a sewing room for Mrs. Lombardi, and a tennis court. Capitalizing on spectacular ocean vistas, Wright placed the majority of the plan on the second floor and cantilevered the living room for a 180-degree view. At the center of this great space is an open fireplace topped by a vent structure and a steeply pitched ceiling perforated by clerestory transom vents. Wright likened the room to a Southwestern Indian tepee and proposed that the hearth be covered with sand and brushed with pattern. The rubble-stone masonry balconies and Cherokee red trim also suggest an affinity with Taliesin West, his father's Arizona home. Although the Lombardis approved Wright's design, the Palos Verdes Art Jury mandated changes: red clay tile replaced blue tile for the roof, and the clerestory windows and overhangs were made smaller. When Wright offered to oversee construction, John Lombardi wrote, "Having waged a successful battle to preserve the 'Wright creation' in the halls of the Art Jury we have always felt that total supervision by yourself would insure total creativity in the manner you intended." And so he did.

1 View from street **2** View from driveway

1 View toward living room at night
2 Drawing, c.1965

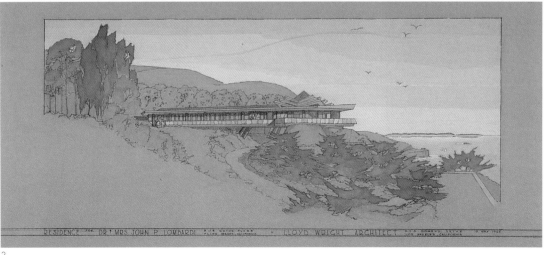

1 Living-room terrace detail

2 Roof detail

3 Clerestory transom vents

4 Living room

5 Fireplace hood with
Lloyd Wright in silhouette

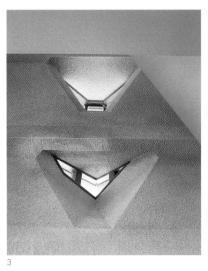

LLOYD WRIGHT'S STUDIO

A Son's Reflections by Eric Lloyd Wright

LW, FLW, and ELW at Wingspread, c.1937

CLOCKWISE FROM TOP LEFT: Lloyd, 10 months, c.1891; Lloyd, age 4, c.1894; Lloyd, age 8, c.1898; Lloyd, age 14, c.1904

I left my grandfather's studio in 1956 and went to work for my father at his home and studio, a two-story house on a small corner lot on the east side of Doheny Drive in West Hollywood. The other side of Doheny, which is part of Beverly Hills, is lined with larger houses and city lots than the West Hollywood side. When I was a boy, the west side of the street consisted of a series of bean fields; and West Hollywood was a collection of small houses occupied by the streetcar motormen, conductors, and other employees of Pacific Electric Railway. When I returned in 1956, the streetcars were giving way to buses, and the conductors and motormen were being replaced by actors, artists, and young professionals. West Hollywood was moving up the urban ladder, and Doheny Drive had become a very busy street. My father had anticipated the urban development of the bean fields, but he had hoped that instead of houses a park would be planted, like that along Santa Monica Boulevard.

My father turned his house in on itself. Because it was on a corner lot, he had just two adjacent lot lines, so he needed only a five-foot setback on the sides and fifteen-foot setback lines on the two streets. He brought the house and studio out to the setback lines and created a courtyard on the Vista Grande side, which he enclosed within an eight-foot wall and opened into the studio. This gave him open space outside of the studio but provided protection from the street. Perforated concrete blocks in front of the exterior windows allowed people inside to look out while preventing people on the sidewalk or street from seeing in. The studio was at street level and the residence upstairs; each floor had a separate entry.

Two pine trees dominated the lot: a huge Italian stone pine grew out of the studio court and a large Aleppo pine grew out of a raised planter on Doheny Drive. When he was in college, my father went with my grandfather to Italy to work on drawings for the Wasmuth portfolio of my grandfather's work. There my father admired the magnificent umbrella-headed pines growing out of the villas and along the Appian Way, and he promised himself that when he built his own house he would plant a stone pine.

The tree lived to be more than seventy years old—with a trunk five feet in diameter—only to die a few years ago. One of my fondest memories is of being in what my father called the "great room," which opened out into the studio courtyard. From there I could see the magnificent pine's trunk reaching up and out of the court; it was equally impressive from the second-floor living room, over which the pine spread its branches.

My father's office consisted of the great room, court, a small entryway, and in the studio, his room with a secretarial space, a bathroom, and two small drafting rooms. We used the garage to store blueprints, dead files, and building materials samples.

When I came back to work in the office, my father's secretary was Mabel Steinmell, who had been with him for twenty years and stayed into her seventies, and two draftsmen, Robert Marks and Johnny O'Neill. At the time they were working on a residence for Dr. Louis Moore in Palos Verdes, a Visitor's Center for the Wayfarer's Chapel, and an amphitheater and cafeteria for the Institute of Mentalphysics. The office staff generally consisted of my father, his secretary, and two draftspeople, but could expand to as many as seven depending on the needs of the projects at hand. The small size of the staff allowed the draftspeople to participate in a wide range of work, from perspective preliminaries to working drawings and job supervision. It was a marvelous opportunity to learn about all aspects of architecture.

My father worked closely with his staff. He would handle the initial work with a client, drawing freehand sketches of the floor plan, plot plan, and elevation, later developing the sketches with a T-square and triangle. He would then give these sketches to a draftsperson to develop further, after which he would modify and correct it. The draftsperson would set up a perspective of the building from a thumbnail sketch my father had made indicating the direction from which the view of the building should be taken. My father usually did the rendering of the perspective; the staff drew up the preliminary presentation drawings of the floor plans, sections, and elevations.

When the sketches were given to the staff, we would set up a unit system chosen by my father and fit the floor plan into that system. This helped to maintain the proportions of the building. Often the sketches started on the back of an envelope or a scrap of writing paper. Once he sketched out an idea on a cloth napkin in a restaurant and persuaded the waiter to let him keep it.

After the owner approved the sketches, the staff would set them up into working drawings, with my father checking the work periodically to ensure that the original concept was maintained and making modifications as structural or budgetary conditions dictated. He would also take the lead in designing the details, which to him were almost as important as the general concept.

When I first joined the office, my father handled building permits and job supervision, but later he shifted more of these duties to the staff.

The office staff also handled the structural engineering on residences, which was originally managed by Bob Marks until I took it over. I also took on the task of getting plans through the Building Department and supervising jobs, so that my father could devote more time to designing and working on theoretical ideas, such as city and county planning, as well as giving lectures and answering requests for information about his father and himself. Toward the end of his life, I even took over doing more of the renderings.

It was a close-knit office and pressures could run high, especially when we had a deadline to meet. It was not unusual to work until ten or eleven at night for several days in a row to get a project out. This put stress on everyone, particularly my father, who had a short temper (a trait he inherited from his father).

My father was the oldest of six children and often had to take charge of his siblings, who were rebellious by nature. This, along with his red hair, made for a quick temper. He could be devastating in his anger, which often diminished as suddenly as it had appeared. After many of his tirades he would survey the devastation around him and ask what was wrong: Why were people feeling so hurt? Those closest to him suffered his anger most. For example, he often expected the draftspeople to have as much knowledge and understanding as he had; but of course we always fell short. His temper could get him into trouble not only with his staff but also with the contractors and clients. My brother once said that if my father had been a painter he could have taken out his frustrations on the canvas. But as an architect, he had to sublimate them to the harmony of the space he was creating in a building.

I believe that the frustration he felt at not being able to realize all the wonderful designs he had in his fertile mind, because of the restrictions by clients and contractors—coupled with his own volatile nature—led him to prefer to do his own renderings. This gave him some outlet for the creative energy that was not always fulfilled in his buildings. And he was a master renderer. He liked to work in carbon pencil and tempera washes on mat board. He would also make colored pencil renderings, often combining the pencil with tempera on tracing paper. In his tempera renderings, he would achieve great depth with very few colors. Some renderings had only two sparingly used color washes and carbon pencil, yet they seemed alive with color. I believe he learned this technique through studying Japanese prints and screens, as well as Chinese paintings. He had a superb sense of space—of when to let "emptiness" alone speak.

CLOCKWISE FROM TOP LEFT: Lloyd, age 20, c.1910; Lloyd in his early 30s, c.1920; Christmas card

My grandfather considered my father one of the finest renderers he had ever known. I remember seeing his drawing of San Marcos in the Desert hanging over my grandfather's desk in his office at Taliesin West. My grandfather pointed to it once and said to me: "Eric, that's the best thing your father's ever done." I didn't know whether to take it as a compliment to my father or not, because what came to my mind was: "What about all the beautiful buildings he designed?" But then that might have been asking too much of such a strong ego. As was true of his son, my grandfather's expectations of those close to him were the highest, and living up to them was difficult—if not impossible.

Christmas cards provided my father with another art form through which to express his creative nature. He loved to design them, and his concepts were highly original. The only problem was that he would start designing the cards only three weeks before Christmas. By the time we got them printed (which was a hectic process), it was usually less than a week before Christmas. Eventually we omitted the "Merry Christmas" and "Happy Holidays" and had them read "Happy New Year."

A card that I liked particularly had an abstract tree in the center-fold, with the upper corners folded back. It was embossed in gold with a perforated pattern in the center, through which a sprig of juniper was inserted. I remember visiting Taliesin a year or so later and seeing this card displayed prominently in the room of Gene Masselink, who was a superb artist and my grandfather's personal secretary.

One of my father's great strengths was his knowledge of landscape architecture. Having been a landscape architect before becoming an architect gave him the ability to integrate landscape into a building design. He would explore the nature of growing things and apply the principles of organic growth to the architecture of the building. He made a landscape plan for every one of his buildings. Even if the clients couldn't afford to have him design the furnishings, he usually talked them into following his landscape plans. They were always part of the working drawing package, whether the client asked for them or not.

My father loved to design furniture. He was able to do this in some of his early houses, but as time went by it became too expensive for most owners. And the amount of time it took to get working drawings completed and through the Building Department increased, making it difficult to get furniture drawings out as well. One later house for which he was able to design the furniture was the Bowler residence.

My father also had a deep love of music; some of his most enduring client relationships were with musicians and composers: Gregor

Piatigorsky, Jascha Heifetz, Warwick Evans, Louis Kaufman, and Alfred Newman, to name just a few. My father loved to attend musical evenings at their houses. One of the loveliest interiors he designed for any client was the studio room for Heifetz in Beverly Hills. His Hollywood Bowl shells also evidence his interest in music and knowledge of acoustics.

When I was in high school my father played the cello, my brother the viola, and I played the flute. We used to perform chamber music once or twice a month. When I came back to work in the office, we generally played on a weekly basis. It was one of my father's most treasured forms of recreation.

In the 1940s and '50s he became quite involved in applying musical notation to color and form. He designated different colors for particular notes; the more intense the color, the louder. He first transcribed the compositions of well-known composers into colored patterns. The most interesting patterns were those of Bach. They were very close to the geometric abstractions made by my father and grandfather. After he had transcribed several composers to perfect his color tones, my father made his own colored abstraction on musical notation paper, which he then transcribed into musical notes. Once we got some of our friends together to play the score. It was very beautiful, and we all were amazed at how well it worked. The process took a great deal longer than to compose a piece of music directly in musical notation; but it demonstrated a relationship between sound and visual image.

When I worked with my father, I noticed that he was a stickler for detail, both in the office and on-site. This appealed to many of his clients, especially perfectionists like Heifetz. It was hard on the office force, however, because we had to spend a lot of time working out details, both on the board and out on the job, knowing that we would get hell if things were not just "Wright."

I can remember my father drawing details on two-by-fours when he didn't have a piece of paper. In the 1930s and '40s labor was cheap, and an architect could spend time on the job drawing up last-minute details of what needed to be done. The carpenters were not only inexpensive but they knew what they were doing; they didn't have to be instructed at every turn. As the cost of construction labor rose and the skills of the tradesmen—especially carpenters—declined, we had to do more detailing in the office prior to construction. Modifications on jobs began necessitating Change Orders for more money, making the owner unhappy and creating tension between my father and the contractor over what was in the contract and on the plans. Every successive set of

TOP: Helen Taggart (Eric's mother), Maginel (Lloyd's aunt), and Eric Wright. BOTTOM: Lloyd, 1940s

LEFT TO RIGHT: Lloyd, age 72, 1962; Lloyd, age 86, 1976

drawings seemed to have more sheets. When I started working for my father, a set of drawings for a residence usually consisted of about eight to ten sheets; toward the end of his life, we were turning out twenty to twenty-four sheets per residence.

My father's office was more than one of business: it was a design studio. Creative designs were the core of the practice—a true wedding of art, engineering, planning, construction techniques, business, and relationships. Business and relationships were the least integrated into studio life. Like many architects, my father was often so eager to do a job that he would lower his fees, and he always put so much time into a job that he would sometimes end up paying the client for the privilege of working on a project! Indeed most of the time it was a scramble to keep the office going financially. On occasion my father even sent me out to collect money from clients because cash flow was so tight.

While I worked with him, my father designed eight churches, of which only one, the Wayfarer's Chapel, was completely built. Two of them—the First Christian Church of Thousand Oaks, California, and the Good Shepherd Community Church of Des Plaines, Illinois—were only partially built, with the main structures never started. These were some of his finest designs, but because of tight budgets and/or a lack of understanding between the building committees and my father, the churches were not built. Committees were difficult for my father to deal with. He was much more comfortable with individuals. In the case of the Wayfarer's Chapel, two women—Elizabeth Schellenberg and Narcissa Cox Vanderlip—made construction possible. Mrs. Schellenberg conceived the idea of a church where people out on a Sunday drive could stop and have a few moments of repose, and Mrs. Vanderlip shared this vision, supplying the land and money.

There were a few exhibitions of my father's architecture when I worked for him. He had a show of drawings and photographs at the University of Oklahoma that was organized by Dean Vollendorf, and one in Los Angeles at the Architects and Engineers Service Building Center. His biggest show probably was the one arranged by David Gebhard and Harriette Von Breton at the University of California at Santa Barbara.

Dad had a concept for this show: he saw it as a total experience of space, not just the viewing of pictures. He redesigned the entrance to the gallery with concrete textile blocks whose patterns were taken from his home and studio. There was an open courtyard at one end of the gallery, in which my father made sculptures and a pool out of the Beverly

Johnson residence concrete blocks. The interior gallery space was furnished mainly with pieces from various houses and a large photo mural of some of his major works, such as the Hollywood Bowl, Bowler house, and Wayfarer's Chapel. He also had models of the Catholic Cathedral and several other buildings.

I remember that David and Harriette wanted to include drawings and more photographs; and when we had just started to hang the show, my father got so upset that he threatened to call the whole thing off. Fortunately Harriette and I were able to calm him down, and a compromise was reached regarding what was to be included. My father had to let go of his desire for a 30-foot-high pendulum in the courtyard, as well as other sculptures and partitions made from patterned concrete blocks from various houses. By the time they finished the block work in the entry and courtyard, as well as the landscaping in the court, the exhibition was over budget. However, David was able to get speakers mounted in various parts of the gallery so there would be a musical background to further integrate the arts into a total concept. Despite the compromises, it was a wonderful show.

But as badly as my father needed publicity and the exposure of his buildings, he was always more interested in making a creative statement. I remember when the architect Sky Brown wanted to do a series of video interviews with him. Difficulties arose when my father insisted on having large murals of his buildings made to use, along with concrete-block screens and fabric with an abstract pattern, as a background. All of this was beyond Brown's financial means, so the project died because Dad would not do just a simple interview.

A similar incident happened when the architectural historian Kathryn Smith wanted to compile an oral history. After three sessions and several hours of taping, Dad scrapped the whole thing because he didn't like the sound of his voice. As a result, there are no videos and very few tapes of my father speaking about his work and philosophy.

For those of us with patience enough to survive my father's quick temper, working with him provided a unique experience in the world of architecture. We were constantly in the midst of creative ferment. Drawing perspectives, rendering preliminary plans, doing working drawings, and supervising jobs as well as setting up exhibitions, designing landscapes, and doing city and regional planning—with my father at the center of it all—could be stressful but never dull.

This book illustrates something of the creative energy my father generated in his studio. His place in the world of architecture and art has not been fully appreciated. His is a contribution to architecture that needs to be seen and understood by a wider audience. Because of him the world of architecture is richer and more creative and—although many of his most original projects were not realized—the seeds of his ideas have been planted and await germination from those of us practicing architecture now and in the future.	□

RESIDENCE   CASCADE   FOR   MR & MRS R E BABCOCK   SAN DIEGO   LLOYD WRIGHT ARCHIT
            VIEW   CALIF.   LOS ANGELES CALIF - RDK

COMPLETE LIST OF **BUILDINGS AND PROJECTS**

Babcock House, San Diego, California, 1953

COMPLETE LIST OF BUILDINGS AND PROJECTS

The following list comprises buildings, landscape plans, and projects that Wright designed. It does not include all the works from the period prior to his independent practice. Works are arranged chronologically by dates of design. Numbers in parentheses come from Wright's job file system. Projects in boldface denote a built work. Multiple dates and job numbers indicate subsequent commissions.

1915   **John L. Severence Estate**, Landscape design with Paul Thiene, Pasadena, California 1915–16

          Ben Meyer Estate, Landscape design with Paul Thiene, Beverly Hills, California 1915–16

1917   Mrs. S. M. B. Hunt House II, Landscape design for Frank Lloyd Wright house, Oshkosh, Wisconsin

1919   **Barnsdall (Hollyhock) House**, Perspective renderings, landscape design, construction supervision of Frank Lloyd Wright house, Olive Hill, Hollywood, California 1919–20

1920   Phoenix Country Club, Landscape design, Phoenix, Arizona (#1)

          W. J. Dodd Estate, Landscape design, Beverly Hills, California (#2)

1921   **Kenneth Preuss Estate**, Landscape design, Laughlin Park, Hollywood, California (#3)

          W. J. Weber House, 3923 West 9th Street, Los Angeles, California (#4)

          Santa Monica High School Open-Air Theater, Landscape design, Santa Monica, California (#6)

1922   **University Club**, Landscape design, Los Angeles, California (#5)

          Martha Taggart House, Including landscaping, 2158 Live Oak Drive, Los Angeles, California (#7) 1922, 1924

          Lyman Gage Development, Landscape design, Sierra Madre, California (#8)

Otto Bollman House, 2200 Broadview Terrace, Hollywood, California (#9)

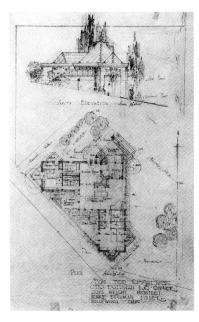

The Otto Bollman house exemplifies Wright's objective to create a design unique to each project. Bollman was the brother of Wright's contractor, Henry Bollman, who built this singular house. The texture and color of the house's original materials—dressed board and wooden shakes applied in alternating courses painted blue and jungle green—animated its exterior, creating an allover geometrical pattern. The plan, which consists of two rectangular wings that intersect a central square on angle, reflects Wright's interest in rotation and diagonal orientation as a means of form-making. He made ingenious use of the entire site by rotating the plan 45 degrees and extending the wings to the property's edge. The resulting outdoor spaces are filled with terraces, gardens, and balconies. Although the exterior has been greatly altered over the years, the interior still suggests the house's dynamic spatial qualities and jaunty ornamentation.

1922   **Henry O. Bollman House**, 1530 Ogden Avenue, Hollywood, California (#10)

1923   Doheny Ranch Resort, Landscape design for Frank Lloyd Wright project, Beverly Hills, California

Sierra Madre City Park, Landscape design competition, Sierra Madre, California (#13)

Dr. John Storer House, Landscape design, construction supervision for Frank Lloyd Wright house, 8161 Hollywood Boulevard, Hollywood, California (#17)

1924   **Charles W. and Mabel Ennis House,** Landscape design, construction supervision for Frank Lloyd Wright house, 2607 Glendower Avenue, Los Angeles, California (#14)

Samuel and Harriet Freeman House, Landscape design, construction supervision for Frank Lloyd Wright house, 1962 Glencoe Way, Hollywood, California (#15)

Oasis Hotel, 125 Palm South Canyon Drive, Palm Springs, California (#16) (altered) 1923–24

For Wright's first major commercial work—a 20-room hotel, dining room, and shops built around a large courtyard—he devised an innovative slip-form system, in which workmen poured concrete in 12-inch courses. The process proved to be costly and time-consuming and resulted in roughly finished walls. Even so, the client, Pearl McCallum McManus, recalled, "It took a year to complete and was so beautiful that many people offered to buy it or lease it before it was finished."

Ellen True Rookery Tents, Palm Springs, California (#18) (not extant)

Mausoleum

1925   **Herbert Howe House,** 513 Roxbury Drive, Beverly Hills, California (#20)

Dr. J. K. Gilkerson House, Landscape design, Glendale, California (#21)

Harry and Alice E. Carr House, 3202 Lowry Road, Los Angeles, California (#22)

City of Oshkosh, Landscape design, Oshkosh, Wisconsin (#23)

John Stahl House, Beverly Hills, California (#24)

1925   Civic Center for Los Angeles (#43)

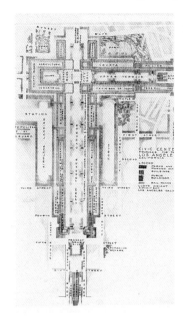

Wright designed the first in a series of urban plans for Los Angeles in response to debates over the city's rapid expansion. Published in the *Los Angeles Times*, this comprehensive plan presented a new skyscraper city, in which modern high-rises, terraced gardens, and modern modes of transportation created a sleek setback composition. The proposal anticipated the implications of remaking a civic center for the metropolitan area in light of the city's identity as a hub of industry and transportation. Integral to the plan were providing links to the harbor, transcontinental railroad, and trucklines, as well as separating types of traffic within the city: underground subways and sunken rapid-transit lines, and high-speed motorways that were channeled through tunnels to eliminate sidewalk parking and congested intersections. To Wright, the plan represented a way to realize "a civic center more magnificent than the hanging gardens of Babylon."

1926   "City of the Future"

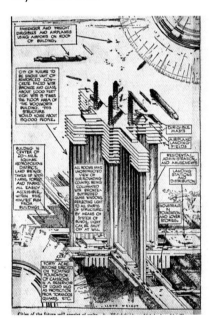

In 1926 Wright launched an audacious urban plan that was heralded as a "Perfect City of Future" by a local newspaper: "The city of the future, rising on the sites of the present crowded, unplanned and unbeautiful metropolises, will be scientifically arranged and esthetically designed structures . . . capable of housing 150,000 persons." Wright envisioned the future city as a cruciform-shaped, 1,000-feet-high reinforced-concrete megastructure with a quake- and tornado-proof floating foundation. It comprised 40 acres of floor area as well as dirigible masts and airplane landing fields. Built in the center of a 20-mile district, this "city" would be surrounded by parks, farms, and forests, all "easily accessible, within five minutes run from buildings."

Alice Millard House, Studio Addition, 645 Prospect Crescent Way, Pasadena, California (#25) 1926, 1932

J. G. Melson House, Los Angeles, California (#26)

1926   **E. E. Calori House,** 3021 Chevy Chase Drive, Glendale, California (#27)

Elliot House, Glendale, California (#29)

Lela Oliver House, Glendale, California (#30)

H. C. Johnson House, Glendale, California (#31)

Fairfax Theater, Fairfax and Santa Monica, Los Angeles, California (#32)

E. R. Lewis House, 2948 Graceland Way, Glendale, California (#33) (remodeled)

1926   **John Sowden House**, 5121 Franklin Avenue, Los Angeles, California (#34)

John D. Derby House, 2601 Chevy Chase Drive, Glendale, California (#35)

Elizabeth Farrell House, 3209 Lowry Road, Los Angeles, California (#36)

Louise (Mrs. W. R.) McDowall House, 2937 Graceland Way, Glendale, California (#47)

Mr. and Mrs. Harry Behn House, Malcolm Avenue, Westwood Hills, California (#73)

S. R. Smith House, Glendale, California (#88)

1927   **Hollywood Bowl**, First shell, Highland Avenue, Hollywood, California (#11) (not extant)

Wright designed the first orchestra shell for the Hollywood Bowl in the shape of a stepped pyramid, which, according to popular lore, was constructed from the discarded materials of a *Robin Hood* set and cost approximately $1,500. The demountable shell could be disassembled easily for pageants and other events, including the traditional Easter service, and received praise for excellent acoustics. Wright said that its form derived from American Indian motifs, but it struck many as too modern and even "startled the conservatives." The next year Bowl management commissioned Wright to design a new shell, this time with a curvilinear form.

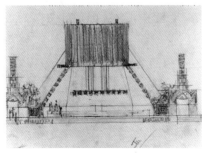

1927   **Lloyd Wright Studio-Residence**, 858 North Doheny Drive, West Hollywood, California (#37) 1927, 1966

Mr. and Mrs. Harry Behn House, Kennington Drive, Glendale, California (#49)

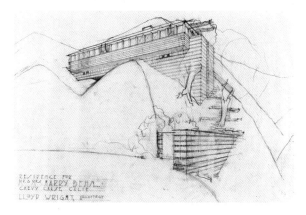

Leerdam Glass Designs (#38)

William Conselman House, 4905 Lockhaven Avenue, Eagle Rock, California (#39)

Will Connell House, 335 North Berendo Street, Los Angeles, California (#40)

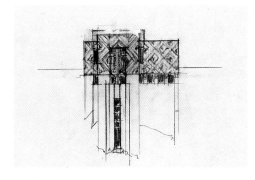

Wilkes Theatre and Shops, Hollywood, California (#41)

1927   Grover Jones House, Brentwood, California (#42)

Burn Martin Ranch House, Palm Springs, California (#44)

Tent (Dune) House, Palm Springs, California c.1927

Lake Arrowhead Hotel and Bungalows, California c.1927–28

1928   **Jake Zeitlin Bookshop,** Shelves, 567 South Hope Street, Los Angeles, California c.1927 (not extant)

Milton Metzler House, Camarillo, California (#45)

Mrs. Frank H. Upman House, Additions and landscape design, 1943 Mendocino Lane, Altadena, California (#46)

O. Meadows House, Laurel Canyon Park, California (#46B)

Samuel-Novarro House, 5609 Valley Oak Drive, Los Angeles, California (#50, 50a) 1928, 1931

1928   **Yucca-Vine Market for Raymond Griffith**, 6327 Yucca Street, Hollywood, California (#51) (demolished)

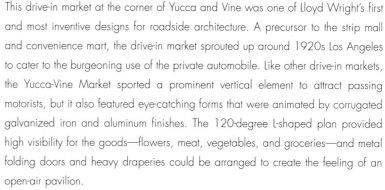

This drive-in market at the corner of Yucca and Vine was one of Lloyd Wright's first and most inventive designs for roadside architecture. A precursor to the strip mall and convenience mart, the drive-in market sprouted up around 1920s Los Angeles to cater to the burgeoning use of the private automobile. Like other drive-in markets, the Yucca-Vine Market sported a prominent vertical element to attract passing motorists, but it also featured eye-catching forms that were animated by corrugated galvanized iron and aluminum finishes. The 120-degree L-shaped plan provided high visibility for the goods—flowers, meat, vegetables, and groceries—and metal folding doors and heavy draperies could be arranged to create the feeling of an open-air pavilion.

Hollywood Bowl, Second shell, Hollywood, California (#11) (not extant)

For the second Hollywood Bowl orchestra shell, Wright assembled a series of hollow wooden rings, tautly bound together with steel rods and turnbuckles for tension. With the flat surfaces of the rings angled directly above the orchestra for reflection and distribution, it resonated like a stringed instrument. Like the first shell, this one was demountable and meant to be stored during the rainy winter months. Without proper storage, the wooden shell became damaged and in 1929 Bowl management hired the Allied Architects to replace it with an all-steel shell.

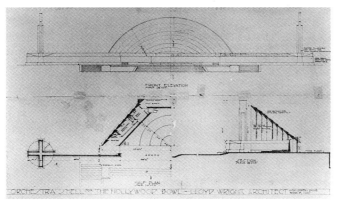

1928   Los Angeles Municipal Airport at Mines Field   1928–29

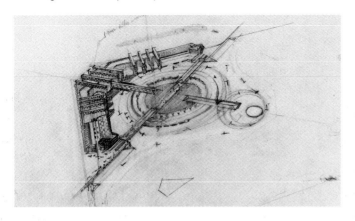

1929   Concrete-Block House

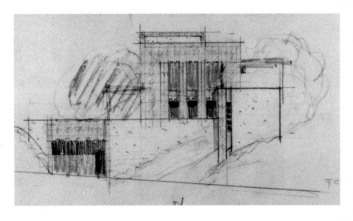

Mrs. Dorothy Bassett House, Landscape design, Los Angeles, California (#52)

Carrol Jones Furniture, Los Angeles, California (#53)

Will O. Backman Store Building, Ventura Boulevard, Tarzana, California (#54)

Albert Marple Stores, Remodel, Los Angeles, California (#55)

Five-Room House, Glendale, California (#56)

1929   Five-Room House, Los Angeles, California

Boeing Airport, Hollywood Way, Burbank, California (#61)

Lehigh Airports Competition Entry

Because Wright was fascinated by aviation technology—he worked for two aircraft companies during World War I—airports and airplanes were crucial features of his urban plans. In 1928 he began to design airports and in the next two years completed three separate schemes, each with a different layout and program. For the Lehigh Airports Competition, Wright drew a central circular landing area surrounded by four arcs housing hangars and machine shops. Howard Shubert notes that although Wright did not receive an honorable mention, he surpassed all the competitors in meticulously planning traffic and circulation patterns, and providing transportation links to the city beyond.

Jake Zeitlin Bookshop, 705½ West 6th Street, Los Angeles, California (#62) (not extant)

In the 1920s Lloyd Wright became affiliated with the journal *Opinion*, for which book dealer Jake Zeitlin served as business manager and recording secretary. Among the Zeitlin social circle (and later Wright clients) were journalist Phil Townsend Hanna, photographer Will Connell, opera singer Lawrence Tibbett, agent and book dealer Louis Samuel, and graphic artist Grace Marion Brown. Wright designed bookshelves for Zeitlin's first bookstore on Hope Street and a year later, when Zeitlin moved to a larger space, the interior of the "At the Sign of the Grasshopper" bookstore and gallery.

1930   **Mr. and Mrs. Richard W. Day House**, Remodel, 2049 Oakstone Way, Los Angeles, California (#57, 95)
1930, 1934, 1936, 1941

Mrs. Lawrence Tibbett House, Remodel, 933 Rexford Drive, Beverly Hills, California (#58)

Office Building, Yucca and Vine Street, Hollywood, California (#60)

Harold Swartz House, Los Angeles, California (#64)

Light Fountain Dedicated to the Motion Picture Industry, Harold Swartz, sculptor; Lloyd Wright, architect (#64)

L. D. Owens Store, Hollywood, California (#65)

1931   Market for Conrad Nagel, Beverly Hills, California   (#66)

Open-Air Theater for Children, Barnsdall Park, Hollywood, California   (#67)

Catholic Cathedral, Los Angeles, California   (#68)

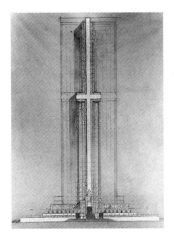 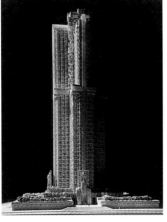

Commissioned by the artist Marguerite Brunswig to design a new cathedral for the Los Angeles Diocese, Wright proposed perforated concrete block as the skin for the entire building and thoroughly integrated the shape of the cross into the design. The intricate patterns of the blocks created cross-shaped perforations, each elevation of the church in turn formed a cross, and its overall plan was a Greek cross. The project was never realized. In 1955 Marguerite Brunswig Staude worked with the architects Anshen and Allen to build the Chapel of the Holy Cross in Sedona, Arizona.

Lois Kellogg Ranch Development, Banning, California   (#69)

1932   Mr. and Mrs. Jules Furthman House, Addition, Los Angeles, California   (#70)

Burt Richardson House, 1849 Campus Road, Eagle Rock, California   (#71)

1932 H. J. Halfhill Apartment Building (#72)

1933 **Jobyna Howland House**, Remodel, 502 Crescent Drive, Beverly Hills, California (#74) 1933–34

Phil Townsend Hanna House, St. Andrews Drive, Glendale, California (#75)

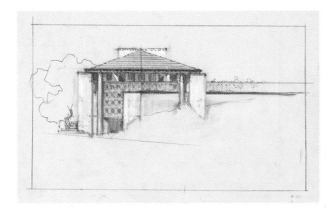

C. R. Henderson Gymnasium, Apollo Baths, Los Angeles, California (#76)

Folding Dog Kennel for Mr. Barnett (#78)

Tule Mat House, Imperial Valley, California (#79)

1934   **Tone Price and Gladys Barbieri Bookshop and Bindery**, Interior remodel, 9045 Sunset Boulevard, Hollywood, California (#80)

Mr. and Mrs. Marks House, Remodel, 710 Hillcrest, Beverly Hills, California (#81)

Alfred Newman House, Remodel, 627 North Canon Drive, Beverly Hills, California (#82)

Cascades Club for J. D. and Dorothy Bassett, Palm Springs, California (#83)

Mrs. Jesse M. Murphy Ranch, Additions, 2800 Rustic Canyon, Pacific Palisades, California

Mrs. Grace Samuel House, 579 North Bundy Drive, Los Angeles, California (#84)

1934   Will Connell House, Remodel and furniture, 335 North Berendo Street, Los Angeles, California (#85)

1935   Mr. and Mrs. Kenneth Niles House, 2601 Rutherford Drive, Los Angeles, California (#86)

Westlake Medical Building, 676 Westlake Avenue, Los Angeles, California (#87) (demolished)

Mr. and Mrs. Louis Kaufman House, 835 Westholme Avenue, Westwood, California (#89, 257, 278) 1935, 1957, 1959

Dr. W. E. Sauer House, Additions, 6309 McPherson Street, St. Louis, Missouri (#90)

Claudette Colbert House, with Ralph Jester, 615 North Faring Road, Beverly Hills, California (#91)

Raymond Griffith House, Laughlin Park, California

Stephen Avery House, 365 Rockingham Avenue, Los Angeles, California (#102) 1935–37

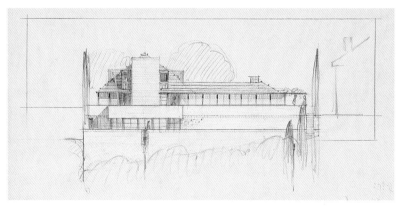

Jake Zeitlin Bookshop, 614 West 6th Street, Los Angeles, California (not extant)

1936   **Mr. and Mrs. Raymond Griffith Ranch House**, 4965 Rigoletto Street, Woodland Hills, California (#92)

1936   Theta Chi Fraternity Building, Westwood, California (#96)

Mr. and Mrs. C. Warwick Evans House, 12036 Benmore Terrace, Los Angeles, California (#99) 1936, 1941

1937   Mr. and Mrs. S. M. Lazarus House, 4966 Ambrose Avenue, Los Angeles, California (#97)

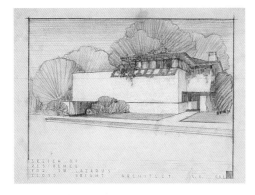

Motor Court (#98)

Mr. and Mrs. Roger Edens House, Remodel, 304 South Cliffwood Drive, Los Angeles, California (#100)

Pern (Mrs. Otto) Brower House, 523 Chapala Drive, Pacific Palisades, California (#101)

Mr. and Mrs. David Gracy House, Austin, Texas (#103)

Harry Ruby House, Addition, 805 North Rodeo Drive, Beverly Hills, California (#104)

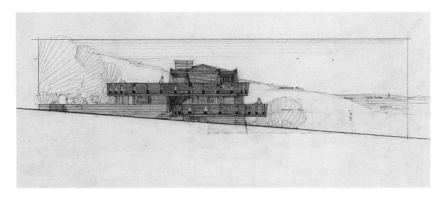

1937   Mr. and Mrs. Felix Jones House, Valley Street, Burbank, California (#105)

Mr. and Mrs. Charles Butterworth House, Parkwood Drive, Beverly Hills, California (#106)

Mr. and Mrs. George Haight House, 1850 Sunset Plaza Drive, Los Angeles, California (#107)

Mr. and Mrs. Charles Vidor House, Briarcrest Drive and Alto Cedro Drive, Los Angeles, California (#111)

1938   Henry F. Henrichs Press Building, Litchfield, Illinois (#108)

Walter Beachy Farm Group (#109)

H. H. van Benthuysen House, Remodel, 937 South Masselin Avenue, Los Angeles, California (#110)

Frances Blalack House, Los Angeles, California (#112)

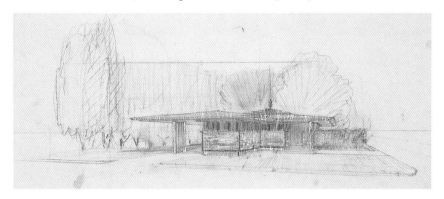

Chair Design (#113)

Christian Science Church, with William Gray Purcell, Monrovia, California (#114)

1939   William A. Smith House, Los Angeles, California (#115)

Mr. and Mrs. George Haight House, Remodel, 613 North Beverly Drive, Beverly Hills, California (#116)

Mr. and Mrs. Jascha Heifetz House, 18 Harbor Island, Newport Beach, California (#117) (not extant)

1939   **W. M. Adams House**, 7400 Tampa Avenue, Reseda, California (#118)

Four-Square Unit Housing, Los Angeles, California (#119)

Film Storage Vault for Cavalier Productions Inc., Burbank, California (#121)

1940   Mr. and Mrs. Harold Swann House, Hope Ranch, Santa Barbara, California (#122)

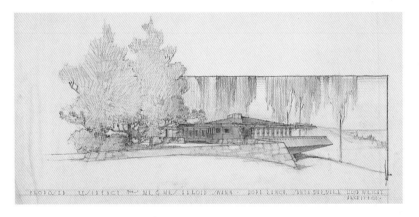

Mr. and Mrs. Armin Degener House, 3374 Deronda Drive, Los Angeles, California (#123)

1940   **Ramona Gardens Public Housing Project**, with George Adams, Ralph Flewelling, Eugene Weston Jr., and Lewis Eugene Wilson; bounded by Murchison, Alcazar, and Indiana Streets, Los Angeles, California (#141) 1940–42

Mr. and Mrs. John Nesbitt House, Remodel of former Ennis House, 2607 Glendower Avenue, Los Angeles, California (#124)

Mrs. Grace Tibbett House, Remodel, 5250 Louise Avenue, Encino, California (#125)

Arch Oboler Roadway and Well Drilling, Prior to construction of Frank Lloyd Wright house, 32436 Mulholland Highway, Malibu, California (#126)

Mr. and Mrs. H. F. Lubsen House, 1262 Rubio Avenue, Altadena, California (#127)

Howard Greer House, 9200 Haskell Avenue, Sepulveda, California (#128, 152, 184) 1940, 1945, 1948

Frederick Othman House, Roof for former Otto Bollman House, 2200 Broadview Terrace, Hollywood, California (#129)

Foiltex, Plans for roof remodel

1941   Nelson Eddy Studio, 485 Halvern Drive, Brentwood Heights, California (#130)

Earl Stendahl House, Interior reconstruction, 7055 Hillside Avenue, Hollywood, California (#131)

Dr. and Mrs. Lionel Lewis House, Remodel, 527 North Crescent Drive, Beverly Hills, California (#132)

Rouben Mamoulian House, Beverly Hills, California (#133)

1941 Mrs. Grace Tibbett Homestead, Bakersfield, California (#134)

Mr. and Mrs. Harold E. Kaye House #1, Remodel, Comstock Avenue, Los Angeles, California (#137)

Lois Kellogg II, Perchino Breeding Farm, Pahrump Valley, Nevada (#138)

Dr. and Mrs. Louis Robinson House, Comstock Avenue, Los Angeles, California (#139)

1942 Demountable Housing, Four-unit plan (#136)

Aliso Village Public Housing Project, with George Adams, Walter Davis, Ralph Flewelling, Eugene Weston Jr., and Louis Eugene Wilson; 1st Street and Mission Road, Los Angeles, California (#140)

The dwindling jobs of the Depression impelled Wright to become active in government-sponsored low-cost housing. But even as the economic climate improved, he stated in 1935 that "low cost housing is as essential for this community as for others," and continued this work through the early 1940s. He lobbied in Washington, D.C., for slum-clearance programs and low-cost housing, and served as the Los Angeles delegate at the International Housing and Town Planning Congress in Mexico City in 1938. As part of Housing Group Architects, Wright worked on Ramona Gardens Public Housing Project, the first low-cost housing project sponsored by the Housing Authority of Los Angeles, and the Aliso Village Public Housing Project. Both consisted of small clusters of low buildings surrounded by lawns, reflecting Wright's opposition to vertical buildings and row houses, and the belief that "every family ha[ve] a piece of ground for their own use."

1944 Olive Hill Site Development, Fine Arts Center, Social Center, Olive Hill Foundation, Medical Arts Center, Educational and Social Science Center, Hollywood, California

George W. Headley House, 2000 North Fuller Avenue, Hollywood, California (#142)

Mr. and Mrs. Frank Jones House, Beverly Hills, California (#143)

Mr. and Mrs. W. B. Tourtellotte House, Palos Verdes, California (#144)

Mr. and Mrs. Warren E. Smith House, Los Angeles, California (#145)

Mr. and Mrs. J. B. (Janet Allen) Schuyler II House, Addition and alterations, 2770 Club Drive, Palms, California (#146)

Fairmont Hotel, Tower addition and remodel, San Francisco, California (#147)

1945 Mr. and Mrs. Floyd Crosby House, Alomar Drive, Studio City, California (#148)

Charles Forsch House, 942 North La Jolla Avenue, Los Angeles, California (#149)

Mr. and Mrs. Harold E. Kaye House #2, Comstock Avenue, Los Angeles, California (#150)

Francisco Cardenas and Mary West 3-C Ranch, Oracle, Arizona (#153)

1945   Mr. and Mrs. L. B. Benjamin House, 1128 Calle Vista Drive, Beverly Hills, California (#154)

Howard Greer Dressmaking Plant, Addition, 8446 West 3rd Street, Los Angeles, California (#156)

Mr. and Mrs. Murray Bothwell House, Ridgeview Drive and Foothill Boulevard, Altadena, California (#157) (status unknown)

1946   Mr. and Mrs. Mel Smith House and Garage, 3146 Haddington Drive, Los Angeles, California (#151)

Institute of Mentalphysics, Caravansary, administration building and site plan, Joshua Tree, California (#158A & B)

Earl Stendahl Candy Factory, Remodel and addition, 710 South Victory Boulevard, Burbank, California (#160)

Frank and Edith Wyle Residential Development, Mulholland Drive, Los Angeles, California (#161)

Mr. and Mrs. David Loew Jr. House, Harlesden Court, Nichols Canyon, California (#159)

Mr. and Mrs. Elias Antaky House, 533 Alta Drive, Beverly Hills, California (#162)

C. T. Kuttler House, Remodel, 866 North Doheny Drive, West Hollywood, California (#163)

Mrs. Forrest Murray House, Remodel, Los Angeles, California (#165)

Mr. and Mrs. Walter Smith House (#166)

Anne Baxter House, Remodel, 8650 Pine Tree Place, Los Angeles, California (#167)

Mr. and Mrs. Ivo Redlich House, 602 North Arden Drive, Beverly Hills, California (#168) (demolished)

Hollyhock House Reconstruction for Olive Hill Foundation, Hollywood, California (#170) 1946–48

Mr. and Mrs. Emanuel Gainsburg House, Including landscaping, 1210 Journey's End Drive, La Cañada, California (#169)

Huntington Hartford Outpost Club, with Frank Lloyd Wright, 2000 North Fuller Avenue, Hollywood, California (#181)

1947   Huntington Hartford Hotel, with Frank Lloyd Wright, 2000 Fuller Avenue, Hollywood, California (#182)

Mr. and Mrs. Kenneth Baxter House, Woodside Hills, San Mateo, California (#172)

Mr. and Mrs. Henry Reitz House, 293 Beverly Glen Boulevard, Westwood, California (#173)

Jane Tibbett House, Florida (#174)

W. E. Dean Carport, 20717 Malibu Road, Malibu, California (#175)

Beatrice Wood Studio and House, Ojai, California (#176)

Swedenborgian Chapel (Wayfarer's Chapel), Portuguese Bend, Palos Verdes, California
(#199, 199A, 229, 243, 287, 341, 362) 1946–58, 1960, 1970, 1977

1948   **Jascha Heifetz House**, Studio addition, 1520 Gilcrest Drive, Beverly Hills, California (#177); subsequent residence remodels: 1951, 1952, 1959, 1961 (#206, 217, 279)

Mr. and Mrs. Ernest Charles House, Pool, terrace and rookery, 1210 Benedict Canyon Drive, Beverly Hills, California (#178)

L. H. Powell House, 9107 St. Ives Drive, Los Angeles, California (#179, 180)

Alma Norton Duffil House, Malibu, California (#185)

Christian Science Reading Room, Fontana, California (#186)

1949   **Mr. and Mrs. Ralph Jester House**, 32 Narcissa Drive, Palos Verdes, California (#187)

Hill and Dale Nursery and Kindergarten School for Mr. and Mrs. Solie Solomon,
Including additions, 16706 Marquez Avenue, Pacific Palisades, California (#188, 209, 268) 1949, 1951, 1953, 1958, 1966

For this progressive preschool on a corner lot in Pacific Palisades, Wright recast the kindergarten as a child's garden. Nestled in a landscape of pine trees and redwoods, the building integrated a pragmatic indoor-outdoor plan with a festive air. The original drawings show clusters of brightly colored geometrical shapes as ornament for the cornice, windows, and flagpole.

Mr. and Mrs. Allan Dorland House, 1370 Morada Place, Altadena, California (#189)

Mr. and Mrs. Alfred Newman House, 14148 Sunset Boulevard, Pacific Palisades, California (#190, 216, 225)
1949, 1951, 1952

Mrs. Frances B. Blalack Apartments, Los Angeles County, California (#191)

J. Welton House, Addition, 859 North Wilcox, Los Angeles, California (#192)

Mr. and Mrs. Jozef Nabel House, 2323 La Mesa Drive, Santa Monica, California (#194, 241, 344) 1949, 1955, 1970

1949   **Mr. and Mrs. P. J. Healy House**, 565 Perugia Way, Los Angeles, California (#196, 212, 219, 283) (not extant) 1949, 1951, 1952

Dr. and Mrs. David Harold Fink House, Mulholland Highway, Los Angeles, California (#197)

T. Leonard Mikules House, Palos Verdes, California (#198)

Huntington Hartford Theater Square, Genesee and Spaulding Avenues at Wilshire Boulevard, Los Angeles, California (#207, 208, 221, 222, 223, 224, 226, 227, 228) 1949–51

1950   **Huntington Hartford Pool Pavilion**, 2001 North Fuller Avenue, Hollywood, California (#200) (not extant)

1950 Mr. and Mrs. Frank W. Jones House, 19818 Lorencita Drive, Covina, California (#201)

Alfred W. Erickson House, 5408 Stauder Circle, Edina, Minnesota (#202)

Arthur Erickson House, 5501 Londonderry Road, Edina, Minnesota (#202)

Dr. and Mrs. Harold Shulman House, 211 Glenroy Place, Los Angeles, California (#203, 218) 1950, 1952 (altered)

Huntington Hartford Foundation Rustic Canyon Projects, Cottages and roads, 2000 Rustic Canyon Road, Pacific Palisades, California (#204)

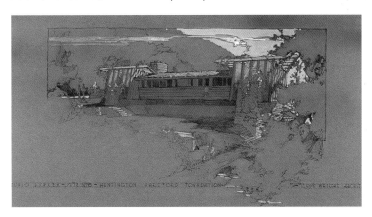

1951 L. N. Schwein House, Remodel of former Raymond Griffith Ranch House, 4965 Rigoletto Street, Canoga Park, California (#205)

Margaret J. (Mrs. Frank) Slater House, North Hiatt Street, La Habra, California (#210)

Seventh Annual City of Los Angeles Art Exhibition, Holmby Park, California (#214)

Snow Chapel, Ile. Bigras, Montreal, Canada (#199A)

1952   **Charles Laughton House**, Pool and dressing room, 1825 North Curson Avenue, Los Angeles, California (#213, 285) (status unknown) 1952, 1960

"John Brown's Body" Traveling Stage Set for Charles Laughton

Mr. and Mrs. Roy A. Kropp House, Chardon Farms, Grayslake, Illinois (#220, 252) 1952, 1956

1953   **Mr. and Mrs. R. V. Honeycutt House**, 5221 Vista Hermosa Avenue, Long Beach, California (#231) 1953–54

Mr. and Mrs. Gordon P. Wagner House, Portuguese Bend, Palos Verdes, California (#232)

Mr. and Mrs. George M. Dell House, 840 Hanley Avenue, Los Angeles, California (#233)

Mrs. Sadie Kanin House, 240 Acari Drive, Los Angeles, California (#234)

Mr. and Mrs. Russell E. Babcock House, Mission Cliff Drive, San Diego, California (#235)

Huntington Hartford Galleries, Hollywood, California (#236) 1953, 1954

After nine years and six projects, only two of which were built, Wright's work for Hartford ended at Runyon Canyon, the site of the Outpost Club (1946) and Huntington Hartford Hotel (1947)—two unrealized projects done in association with his father—and a pool pavilion (1950), which was built. Only after receiving a personal guarantee from Hartford did Wright agree to this commission for painting and sculpture galleries, which would be open to the public. After a year Hartford abandoned this as well, writing, "the loss of time and effort and money has been as much mine as yours." Hartford later hired Edward Durell Stone to build the Gallery of Modern Art (1965) in New York.

1954   **Frank Howard House**, Remodel and additions, 16475 Garvin Drive, Encino, California (#238)

Mr. and Mrs. Eddie Hearn House, Remodel and addition, 10511 Selkirk Lane, Los Angeles, California (#239, 263)
1954, 1957

Institute of Mentalphysics, Cafeteria and cottages, Joshua Tree, California (#240)

1955   Pent-o-Rama House for the Pent-o-Rama Building Company, Arbolado Road, Santa Barbara, California (#242)

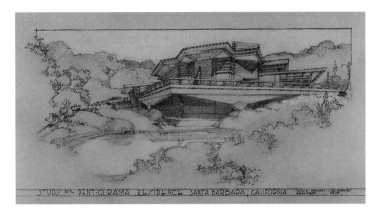

El Cerrito Hillside Church (Community Swedenborgian), El Cerrito, California (#244)

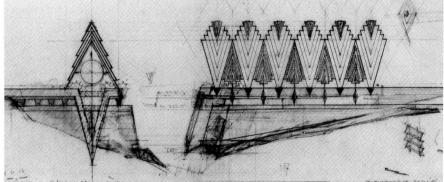

Joshua Tree National Monument Development, Site plan, Joshua Tree, California (#246)

1956   Speaker Resonator (#247)

Robert Childs House, Institute of Mentalphysics, Joshua Tree, California (#248)

Pent-o-Rama House for the Pent-o-Rama Building Company, Angelo Drive, Holmby Hills, California (#250)

Pent-o-Rama House for Armand and Lee Pedicini, Eureka Drive, Los Angeles, California (#251)

1957   Preceptory of Light and Sanctuary for Institute of Mentalphysics, Joshua Tree, California (#253)

Dr. and Mrs. Louis D. Moore House, 504 Paseo del Mar, Palos Verdes, California (#254) 1956, 1957

1957   Mr. and Mrs. Louis Bartfield House, Rolling Oaks Ranch, Ventura County, California   (#258)

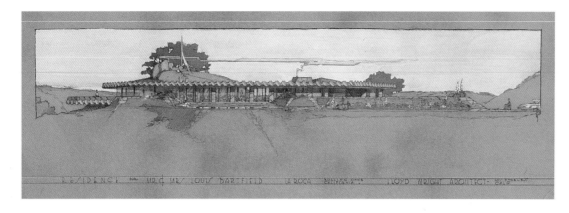

Jacker House, 1265 Oakridge Avenue, Glendale, California   (#259)

Mr. and Mrs. Leonard Polster House, 1098 Hillcrest Road, Beverly Hills, California   (#260)

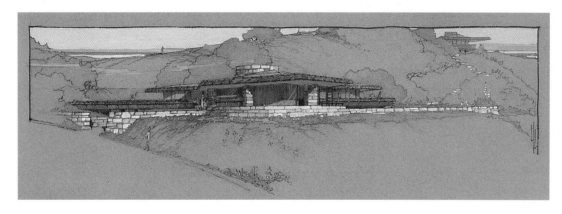

Good Shepherd Community Church, Des Plaines, Illinois   (#262, 272) (not completed)

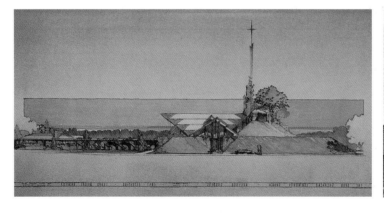

Mr. and Mrs. Rupert Pole Beach House, Malibu, California   (#264)

Frank Howard House, Remodel, 16821 Oak View Drive, Encino, California   (#265)

1958   **Mr. and Mrs. Jack J. Levand House**, 1107 Wallace Ridge Road, Beverly Hills, California (#267)

John L. Mace House, 8292 Hollywood Boulevard, Hollywood, California (#269, 271)

Veda Caroll House, North Beverly Drive, Los Angeles, California (#270)

St. Luke's Presbyterian Church, 26825 Rolling Hills Road, Rolling Hills Estates, California (#273)

 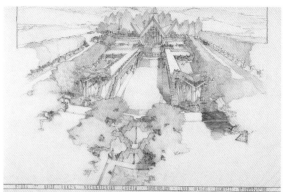

Mr. and Mrs. Lowell Dunham House, Palos Verdes, California (#274)

Barnsdall Park Art Center, Hollywood, California (#276)

1959   **Mr. and Mrs. Gregor Piatigorsky House**, Remodel and addition, 400 South Bundy, Beverly Hills, California (#275, 298, 322) 1959, 1962, 1965

Daniel and Mabel E. DeJonghe House, 9028 Crescent Drive, Los Angeles, California (#195, 281)

Mr. and Mrs. John J. Lumbleau House, 22158 Pacific Coast Highway, Malibu, California (#282)

1960   **Mr. and Mrs. Jacob Karasik House**, 436 Spalding Drive, Beverly Hills, California (#280)

Mr. and Mrs. Ronald Stein House, Granada Hills, California (#284)

Robert Llewellyn Wright House, Landscape design, 7927 Deepwell Drive, Bethesda, Maryland (#306)

1961   **Mr. and Mrs. Charles Pihl House,** Minnetonka, Minnesota (#288, 298) (unsupervised; not built according to LW's design)

Jascha Heifetz Beach House, Malibu Road, Malibu, California (#289)

Mount Olivet Lutheran Church, Additions, 50th Street at Knox Avenue South, Minneapolis, Minnesota (#290)

Herman Steiner Chess Club, Remodel for Mr. and Mrs. Gregor Piatigorsky, 8801 Cashio Street, Los Angeles, California (#291)

Barnsdall Park Art Center/Gallery, Hollywood, California (#354)

Pico-Robertson (Arcade Mall) Shopping Center, Los Angeles, California (#292)

Pilgrimage Play Theater for Hollywood Bowl Association, Remodel for chamber music concerts, Los Angeles, California (#293)

1961   Mr. and Mrs. Louis M. Seeberger House, Remodel, 4661 Vanalden Avenue, Tarzana, California (#295)

Giro Station for Mr. and Mrs. Randolph Galt, Australia (#366)

1962   Huntington Portal, Urban plan, Surfside, California (#297)

Los Angeles County Regional Urban Plan, Los Angeles, California (#299)

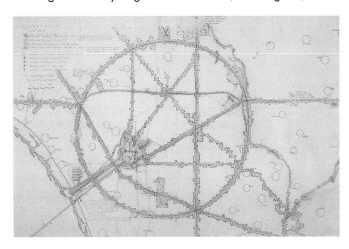

Wright's last regional plan for Los Angeles reflected his growing interest in nature conservation and continued fascination with progressive technologies and transportation, now including rocket ports. This 1962 visionary project presents a freeway and rapid-transit system in which "cluster centers," shown as circles, are connected by transportation arteries to prevent congestion and create a grand parkway. In the accompanying text, he argues for maintaining the unique natural character of the region and asserts that this plan would, among other things, ease labor and promote ethnic integration through automation, transform war-making production into human services, and create "architectural beauty and nobility."

Dr. and Mrs. Robert Hare House, Remodel, 642 Perugia Way, Los Angeles, California (#300)

1963   Mr. and Mrs. Louis Samuel House, (Eric Lloyd Wright, principal designer), Glendower Avenue, Los Angeles, California (#301)

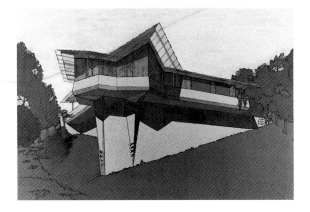

1963   **Mr. and Mrs. John P. Bowler House**, 3456 Via Campesina, Palos Verdes, California (#303, 334) 1963, 1968

Toddao Theatre, Century City, California (#304)

Dr. and Mrs. Leonard A. Harris House, Timken Road, Orange County, California (#305)

Mr. John F. Pfeiffer and Dr. William Hulet House, Granada Road, Coral Gables, Florida (#308)

Beverly Johnson House, 7017 Senalda Road, Hollywood, California (#309)

1964   Terrace Park Apartments for Lincoln Fidelity Corporation, 10842 Magnolia Avenue, Stanton, California (#310)

1964   Student Housing for Lincoln Fidelity Corporation, La Jolla, California (#312)

World Folk Park, Burbank, California (#313)

Moudary-Jowdy House, Remodel of Samuel-Novarro House, 2255 Verde Oak Drive, Los Angeles, California (#314)

Holiday Bargain Fair and Service Station for Erickson Petroleum Corporation, Minneapolis, Minnesota (#315)

1965   Erickson Memorial Garden, Lakewood Memorial Park, Minneapolis, Minnesota (#316)

Church of New Jerusalem and Apartments, 509 South Westmoreland Avenue, Los Angeles, California (#317)

Dr. and Mrs. John P. Lombardi House, 804 Gatos Place, Palos Verdes, California (#318)

Mr. and Mrs. David L. Wright House, Guest house addition, 5212 East Exeter Boulevard, Phoenix, Arizona (#319, 361)
1965, 1977

First Christian Church, Avenida de las Flores, Thousand Oaks, California (#320, 342) 1965, 1970

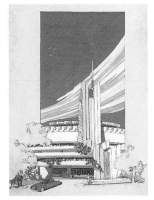  

Alan Handley House, Remodel, 3003 Runyon Canyon Road, Hollywood, California (#321)

1968   **Mr. and Mrs. David Wright Jr. House**, 5226 East Exeter Boulevard, Phoenix, Arizona (#328, 358) 1968, 1977

1968   Dr. S. F. Moorehead House, Addition (pavilion and loggia), 7 Maverick Lane, Rolling Hills, California (#329)

Westfair Shopping Center, Corner of Springdale Street and Warner Avenue, Huntington Beach, California (#330) 1968–69 (not completed according to LW's plans)

Mrs. Louis LaRue House, 35201 Mulholland Highway, Los Angeles, California (#332)

Mr. and Mrs. James Welton House, Remodel, 970 Bel Air Road, Los Angeles, California (#335)

Triangle Park Shopping Center, Remodel for Martin-Fann, Carson Street and Bellflower Boulevard, Long Beach, California (#336) 1969–70

Dr. Richard King Dental Suite, Westfair Shopping Center, Huntington Beach, California (#337)

Hollyhock House, Remodel of gallery complex and fountains, Barnsdall Park, Hollywood, California (#339)

1970   Rev. and Mrs. Robert Alexander House, Thousand Oaks, California (#331)

Unity Temple, Restoration, Oak Park, Illinois (#340, 351) 1970–71, 1973

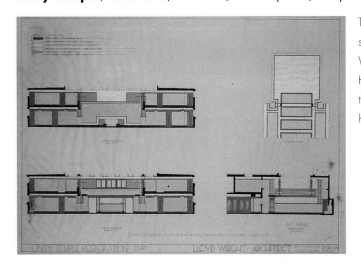

Toward the end of his career Wright became increasingly involved in efforts to preserve and restore his father's buildings, especially Unity Temple and the Frank Lloyd Wright Home and Studio in Oak Park, Illinois, and the Hollyhock House in Hollywood. As a consultant for Unity Temple, he revised the entire color scheme for the parish house using a combination of paint analysis, memory, and knowledge of his father's work.

Dr. Jerome Jacobi House, Remodel of former Storer House, 8161 Hollywood Boulevard, Hollywood, California (#343)

Thanks-Giving Square, Dallas, Texas (#345) 1970–71

1971   **Dr. and Mrs. Leonard Bellenson House**, 410 Capri Drive, Simi Valley, California (#346)

1973   Charles Kasher House, Remodel of former Samuel-Novarro House, 2255 Verde Oak Drive, Los Angeles, California (#349)

George Tomer House, 16321 Kinzie Street, Sepulveda, California (#350)

Los Angeles Central City (Bunker Hill), Proposed Plan (#350.5)

1974   Mr. and Mrs. Burns Henry Jr. House, Glen Oak Hills, Rancho California, California (#352)

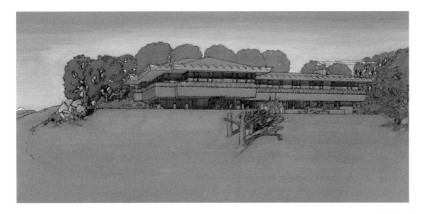

Oak Park Midwest Cultural Center and Frank Lloyd Wright Historic District Park, Oak Park, Illinois (#353)

Hollyhock House and Gallery, Renovation for City of Los Angeles, Barnsdall Park, Hollywood, California (#354) 1974–75

1975   Max Lair House and Solar Farms Subdivision, Granite Mountain, Apple Valley, California (#355)

Robert Llewellyn Wright House, Rug design, 7927 Deepwell Drive, Bethesda, Maryland (#356)

1977   Austin Gardens, Landscape design, Oak Park, Illinois (#362)

David Newman House, 6353 Busch Drive, Malibu, California (#363) 1977–78

1978   Dr. and Mrs. W. E. Crosby House, Remodel, 53 Empty Saddle Lane, Rolling Hills Estates, California (#358)

☐

ARCHIVAL INFORMATION AND PHOTOGRAPHY CREDITS

Most of the archival drawings and photographs were culled from material held by Eric Lloyd Wright and the Department of Special Collections, University Research Library, UCLA. Credit for historical black-and-white photographs are given below to photographers if known.

Bruike Photography: Bowler House aerial view, p. 207
Fred R. Dapprich: Howland House, p. 130 (all)
John Engstead: Studio Portrait of Lloyd Wright, pp. 6, 234 (left)
Floyd Faxon: Catholic Cathedral, pp. 30 (right), 248 (right)
Heifitz Imandt: Lloyd Wright at California Polytechnic State University, p. 234 (right)
Joseph P. Messana: Lloyd Wright, p. 276
The Mott Studio: Newman House, p. 167 (bottom left)
Marvin Rand: Millard Studio, p. 20
Julius Shulman: Wayfarer's Chapel, p. 32; Bowler House, pp. 34, 208 (bottom left), 209 (bottom left), 213 (bottom left), 215 (bottom right);
          Karasik House, pp. 34, 203 (bottom right); Moore House, p. 35; Lombardi House, pp. 35, 227 (bottom right); Aliso Village Public
          Housing Project, p. 256; Redlich House, p. 257 (all); Hill and Dale Nursery, p. 259 (all); Huntington Hartford Theater Square, p. 260
Weiner Photography: Lloyd Wright at Wayfarer's Chapel, pp. 10, 12, 159

Lloyd Wright at home, 1950s

CHRONOLOGY

Most of the information in this chronology comes from primary sources in the University Research Library, University of California, Los Angeles, including correspondence, drawings, and building documents. In addition to public records, contemporary publications and other archival materials, dates for Wright's life before 1919 are based in part on secondary sources.

1890

Frank Lloyd Wright Jr. is born on March 31 in Oak Park, Illinois, eldest son of Frank Lloyd Wright and Catherine Tobin Wright.

1898–1907

Attends Hillside Home School, Spring Green, Wisconsin.

1907–9

Attends University of Wisconsin, Madison.

1909–10

Leaves college in fall to help prepare drawings for his father's Wasmuth publications in Europe; travels in Italy, Germany, and France.

1910

Returns to Chicago and then moves to Brookline, Massachusetts, to work as an architectural draftsman for Olmsted and Olmsted; attends classes at the Harvard botanical gardens and the Arnold Arboretum.

c.1911

Moves to San Diego with his brother John.

1912–13

Works in Irving Gill's office in San Diego as draftsman and landscape architect.

1913

Works as landscape architect in his father's Chicago office at Orchestra Hall.

1915

Begins partnership with landscape architect Paul Thiene in Los Angeles.

c.1916

Joins design department at Paramount Studios in Los Angeles.

1917

Designs *Everyman* stage set for Players Producing Company; marries actress Elaine Hyman (stage name, Kira Markham); works as landscape architect in his father's office in Chicago.

1917–18

Works for Standard Aircraft Co., New Jersey, and Curtis Aircraft, New York; later employed by architects Rouse and Goldstone, and George Chapell, New York.

1919

Moves to Los Angeles to assist with his father's Olive Hill projects for Aline Barnsdall, making renderings and landscape designs, and serving as the first construction supervisor for Hollyhock House.

1920

Works on landscape commissions for architect W. J. Dodd; shares his father's office at the Homer Laughlin Building; completes his first architectural design, Weber House; designs stage sets for *Othello*, Trinity Auditorium (February); and *When We Dead Awaken*, The Little Theater, Los Angeles (April).

1922

Identified as designer of the Martha Taggart and Henry Bollman houses.

1923

Works as landscape architect in his father's office in the house at 1284 Harper Avenue.

1924

Moves office to 5417½ Hollywood Boulevard.

1925

Divorce from Elaine Hyman is finalized.

1926

Marries actress Helen Taggart Pole; becomes stepfather to her son, Rupert, whose father is director Reginald Poel; designs *Julius Caesar* stage set for Gordon Craig, Hollywood Bowl.

1927

Moves into an office-studio and residence at 858 North Doheny Drive; designs *Robin Hood* stage set for Reginald DeKoven's operetta, Hollywood Bowl.

1928

Receives license as architect.

1929

His son, Eric Lloyd Wright, is born on November 8.

1930

Invents color motion-picture process, "A Process for Making Cinematographic Pictures in Color."

1934

Joins architectural team to work on the Utah Street Project, a Public Works Administration housing project. (Part of this team reconvenes in 1940 as Housing Architects Associated to design Ramona Gardens, the first project to be built by the Housing Authority of the City of Los Angeles.)

1938

Serves as delegate at the 16th International Housing and Town Planning Congress in Mexico City, August 13–27.

1940

"Woven and Designed by Maria Steinhof" published in November issue of *California Arts and Architecture*; receives patent on roof and wall surface invention (serial no. 251,074), developed in 1936.

1943

"Aliso Village Group Housing Project Result of Coordinated Planning" published in *Southwest Builder and Contractor*, May 21.

1951

Serves as architectural co-chairman, Seventh Annual City of Los Angeles Art Exhibition, Holmby Park.

1952

Designs *John Brown's Body* traveling stage set for Charles Laughton.

1956

Eric Lloyd Wright joins the Lloyd Wright office.

1962

Travels to Japan with Helen Wright, and Mr. and Mrs. David Wright, April 15–May 25.

1963

"The Individual in Architecture," lecture at California State Polytechnic College at 14th annual awards banquet, April 27.

1964

"The New Dimension, IBM Culture and Urban Ecology," talk given to the Regional Planning and Development section of Town Hall, Biltmore, March 25; an exhibition of Lloyd Wright's architectural work is held at the School of Architecture, University of Oklahoma, Norman, Oklahoma, in April.

1966

The exhibition *Five Decades of Living Architecture: Lloyd Wright, Architect* is presented at Architectural Gallery, Architects and Engineers Service Building Center, Los Angeles, August 8–September 30.

1970

Joins team of three architects contributing to restoration of Frank Lloyd Wright's Unity Temple in Oak Park, Illinois.

1971

The exhibition *Lloyd Wright, Architect: 20th Century Architecture in an Organic Exhibition*, organized by David Gebhard and Harriette Von Breton, is held at the University of California, Santa Barbara, November 23–December 22.

1974–75

Serves as consultant on Frank Lloyd Wright Home and Studio restoration.

1978

After long bout of pneumonia, Wright dies in Santa Monica, California, on May 31.

1986–87

Exhibition of Lloyd Wright drawings presented at GA Gallery, Tokyo, September 20–October 26, 1986; and Max Protetch Gallery, New York, January 6–31, 1987.

BIBLIOGRAPHY

Articles

"Les aeroports á leurs débuts: Trois projets de Lloyd Wright du 12 juin au 16 septembre 1990 (Airport Origins: Three Projects by Lloyd Wright, 12 June–16 September 1990)." Montreal: Centre Canadien d'Architecture, 1990.

"Aliso Village." *California Arts and Architecture* 59 (October 1942): 38–39; (November 1942): 62–63.

Allen, Jennifer. "Claudette Colbert." *Architectural Digest* 47 (April 1990): 226–29.

Beach, John. "Lloyd Wright's Sowden House: Bizarre Shapes from Custom-Cast Concrete Block." *Fine Homebuilding,* no. 14 (April–May 1983): 66–73.

Beardwood, Jack. "Modern Chapel for Wayfarer's." *Collier's* 129 (7 June 1952): 18, 19.

Betsky, Aaron. "Lloyd Wright Recast: Keaton House, Los Angeles, California, Schweitzer, BIM, Architect." *Architectural Record* 179 (September 1991): 126–33.

Buckland, Michael, and John Henken, eds. *The Hollywood Bowl: Tales of Summer Nights*: Los Angeles: Balcony Press, 1996.

Campbell, Liza. "The Surreal Landscape of David Lynch." *House and Garden* 160 (July 1988): 88–93.

"Comprehensive Plan for Los Angeles Beautiful." *Los Angeles Times*, 30 August 1925, pt. 5, p. 4.

Cool, Judy. "Lloyd Wright on Design." *Los Angeles Herald Examiner*, California Living Section, 21 May 1967, p. 10.

"Corrugated Galvanized Iron: Yucca-Vine Market, Hollywood, California." *American Architect* 141 (March 1932): 22–25.

Cutts, A. B., Jr. "The Hillside Home of Ramon Novarro, a Unique Setting Credited by Lloyd Wright." *California Arts and Architecture* 44 (July 1933): 11–13, 31.

Duncan, Michael. "Turn Wright." *Buzz* 9 (March 1998): 102–5.

"Exhibitions: Lloyd Wright, University of California, Santa Barbara." *Architectural Design* 43 (April 1972): 205.

Gibling, Pauline. "Modern California Architects." *Creative Art* 10 (February 1932): 111–15.

Gill, Brendan. "Ramon Novarro: A Screen Idol's Lloyd Wright House." *Architectural Digest* 51 (April 1994): 176–83, 279.

"Glass Roof Lights House Without Windows." *Popular Mechanics* 48 (July 1927): 25.

Goldberger, Paul. "Architecture: In Wright's Shadow." *The New York Times*, 29 January 1987, sec. C, p. 21.

——. "Reorienting a Classic." *Architectural Digest* 44 (March 1987): 108–15.

"Habitation en Californie, Lloyd Wright, Architecte." *L'architecture d'aujourd'hui* 10 (February 1939): 24–25.

Hayeem, Abe. "Not Quite Architecture: FLloyd and Lloyd." *Architects' Journal* 140 (21 October 1964): 897–99.

Hines, Thomas S. "Architecture: Reconsidering Lloyd Wright, A Brilliant Legacy of Residential Design Endures in Los Angeles." *Architectural Digest* 50 (May 1993): 36, 40, 44, 48, 50, 52, 56.

"Howland Residence." *American Architect* 151 (November 1937): 41–42.

"Jake Zeitlin Book Shop, Los Angeles." *Architectural Forum* 67 (September 1937): 192–93.

"John Beach: In Memoriam." *Design Book Review,* no. 9 (spring 1986): 21–23.

Ludlow, Carter. "A Portrait of Lloyd Wright." *Los Angeles Examiner*, 3 November 1961, sec. 2, p. 2.

McCoy, Esther. "Lloyd Wright." *Arts and Architecture* 83 (October 1966): 22–26.

——. "50 Wright Years Iterate Greatness." *Los Angeles Herald Examiner*, 4 September 1966, sec. A, p. 18.

"Needless Damage." *Architectural Forum* 58 (April 1933): 337 and 28 (ad section).

"Newsmakers." *Newsweek* 84 (29 July 1974): 57.

Norrison, Jim. "Architect Lloyd Wright Tells a Dream for L.A." *Citizen-News*, 1977, sec. D, p. 3.

Pastier, John. "Lloyd Wright Retrospective in Channel City." *Los Angeles Times*, 8 December 1971, pt. 4, p. 1.

"Perfect City of Future Is Pictured by Noted Architect." *Los Angeles Evening Herald,* 26 November 1926, pt. 2, p. 1.

Phillips, Patricia C. "Reviews: Lloyd Wright, Max Protetch Gallery." *Artforum* 25 (April 1987): 132.

"Ramona Gardens Housing Project." *Southwest Builder and Contractor* 96 (19 July 1940): 8–13; 97 (16 May 1941): 12–13; 101 (21 May 1943): 12–17.

"Ranch House for Raymond Griffith, Canoga Park, California, Lloyd Wright, Architect." *Architectural Forum* 68 (June 1938): 471–78.

"The Residence of Jobyna Howland, Beverly Hills, California." *California Arts and Architecture* 47 (January 1935): 22–23.

Schindler, Pauline G. "The Samuel House, Los Angeles." *Architectural Record* 67 (June 1930): 525–30.

Shubert, Howard. "Lloyd Wright and the Lehigh Airport Competition." *Revue d'Art Canadienne* 16, no. 2 (1989): 165–70.

"Special Issue: Architect Lloyd Wright—His Life and Work, Articles by Bruce Goff, Masami Tanigawa, Takao Iwazumi, Erik [sic] Wright, and Lloyd Wright." *Space Design* 182 (November 1979): 2–84.

"Studio of Lloyd Wright, Architect, Los Angeles." *Architectural Record* 67 (September 1930): 144.

Viladas, Pilar. "Mimi London: The Continuing Evolution of a Lloyd Wright Home in Los Angeles." *Architectural Digest* 53 (September 1996): 143–55, 236.

"A Visit with the Architect: Lloyd Wright Shares His Architectural Vision of the Wayfarer's Chapel." Rancho Palos Verdes, Calif.: The Wayfarer's Chapel, c.1990.

"War Housing, 610 Permanent Units, Los Angeles." *Architectural Forum* 76 (June 1942): 402–3.

"Wayfarer's Chapel, Palos Verdes, California." *Architectural Forum* 95 (August 1951): 153–55.

Webb, Michael. "Polishing a Jewel by Lloyd Wright." *Architectural Digest* 52 (July 1995): 62–71.

Weston, Eugene, Jr. "Ramona Gardens Housing Project." *California Arts and Architecture* 57 (December 1940): 34–35.

"What Is Art?" *Los Angeles Evening Herald,* 7 March 1929, p. A-3.

Wright, Lloyd. "Aliso Village Group Housing Project Result of Coordinated Planning." *Southwest Builder and Contractor* 101 (21 May 1943): 12–17.

——. "Woven and Designed by Maria Steinhof." *California Arts and Architecture* 57 (November 1940): 19.

Books and Catalogues

Alofsin, Anthony. *Frank Lloyd Wright: The Lost Years, 1910–1922.* Chicago and London: The University of Chicago Press, 1993.

DeLong, David, ed. *Frank Lloyd Wright: Designs for an American Landscape.* New York: Harry N. Abrams, 1996.

Dobyns, Winifred Starr. *California Gardens.* New York: Macmillan, 1931.

Field, Dorothy J. *The Human House.* Boston: Houghton Mifflin Co., 1939

Five Decades of Living Architecture: Lloyd Wright, Architect. Los Angeles: Architectural Gallery, Architects and Engineers Service Building Center, August 8–September 30, 1966.

Gebhard, David, and Harriette Von Breton. *Lloyd Wright, Architect: 20th Century Architecture in an Organic Exhibition.* Santa Barbara: University of California, 1971.

Lloyd Wright. Norman, Okla.: School of Architecture, University of Oklahoma, 1964.

Lloyd Wright Drawings. Tokyo: Yukio Futagawa, 1986.

Meehan, Patrick Joseph. *Lloyd Wright: A Prairie School Architect.* Monticello, Ill.: Vance Bibliographies, 1978.

Onderdonk, Francis S. *The Ferro-Concrete Style.* New York: Architectural Book Publishers, 1928.

Riley, Terence, ed. *Frank Lloyd Wright Architect.* New York: The Museum of Modern Art, 1994.

Smith, Kathryn. *Frank Lloyd Wright: Hollyhock House and Olive Hill.* New York: Rizzoli International Publications, 1992.

Sweeney, Robert L. *Wright in Hollywood: Visions of a New Architecture.* New York: The Architectural History Foundation; London and Cambridge, Mass.: The MIT Press, 1994.

Wright, Frank Lloyd. *An Autobiography.* 3d ed. New York: Horizon Press, 1977.

——. *Ausgeführte Bauten und Entwürfe von Frank Lloyd Wright.* Berlin: Ernst Wasmuth, 1910.